8Acts
23Scenes

nanam

NANAM Publishing House
193 Hoedong-gil, Paju-si, Gyeonggi-do, Korea
(http://www.nanam.net)

Printed in Korea, 2016
ISBN 978-89-300-8817-6
ISBN 978-89-300-8655-4 (Set)

Autobiography, Huh Unna

8Acts
23Scenes

Author Huh Unna

Translator Lisa Sojung Jeon

nanam

I dedicate this book
to my beloved daughter
who lived a lonely life
while I was busy filling the scenes
of my life's 8 acts and 23 scenes,
and to my son
who has always quietly watched
and supported me in all the paths
that I have walked.

Testimonials

Song Young Gil
Mayor of Incheon

8 Acts 23 Scenes! What an amazing life story. Some life stories end within the first two or three acts. So rare are the ones who craft their lives so dramatically across eight acts. More surprisingly, this act is far from being over. Dr. Huh is still preparing a new stage. Possessing ever so much energy and moving through the world like a cloud, I think this expression describes Dr. Huh's life quite well.

I first met Dr. Huh while I was serving as a fellow parliamentarian. It was rare that someone from Gyunggi Girl's Middle School, Gyunggi Girl's High School, Seoul National University, with a PhD from the States and without an activist background had joined our party, and I learned a lot by participating in IPAIT Dr. Huh led. At the time, Dr. Huh was pioneering the new information technology field with her global perspective. Proficient in English, she had contributed greatly to the birth of the Roh Mu Hyun administration. Later, it made a deep impression on me that she never lost her determination or passion despite all the difficulties she faced with different cliques within the party and trying to learn the unfamiliar ways of the politics. I also remember her working with great passion as the president of ICU, working tirelessly to prevent the university from closing down, which was something that was initiated by a member of the opposition party, Young Sun Kim.

After she left the National Assembly, I occasionally heard about her news, but during my third term, we lost contact almost entirely. Then after I became the mayor of Incheon, I found out she was working as the Korean director at Songdo's Chadwick School. I thought, "What a surprising coincidence!"

Chadwick School Songdo was facing various issues that were delaying its opening, and Dr. Huh's relentless efforts finally helped the school open its doors. On the day of the school's opening ceremony, I was invited by Dr. Huh to give a speech as the city's mayor, and I still remember how deeply moved I was that day.

I am very pleased to know that I have shared some of the moments described in this book with Dr. Huh. As well, I am also very thankful that I will be a part of the new chapter of her life that is about to begin in Incheon.

Dr. Huh's girlish innocence and passion, her compassion and kindness for the world, her bold stance against authority and formality, her curiosity and intellectual pursuit of new things are all the virtues she has practiced throughout her whole life. These, as well as her accomplishments serve as motivation and inspiration for countless other women leaders.

I believe that Incheon, the heart of Korea and its economic capital, is a good match for Dr. Huh who possesses international leadership and corresponding passion. With Dr. Huh as the new director at Chadwick School Songdo as well as a member of Incheon's 'Foreign Investment Committee,' I can't wait to see her upcoming life stories that will take place right here in Incheon.

Kim Jong Ryang

Chairman of Hanyang University

I believe the happiest lives are the ones where people live according to their own wishes, on their own personal stage. In this respect, I see Dr. Huh as someone who has written her own great life scenario and directed her own film. She is both the director and the main actress in her own film. Her autobiography is a book that unveils her dramatic life, with many planned and unplanned events she experienced.

In my opinion, the true measure of a life comes not from our accomplishments alone, but from how much meaning and value we have felt and created during our lifetime. In 1985, Dr. Huh and I were leading the Education Technology department at Hanyang University which was all but barren at the time. Dr. Huh had fervent passion and with it, she turned our new department into a prestigious one that it is today. Thanks to her efforts, nowadays, graduates of our department are scattered across major corporations and public institutions, adding even more prestige to the department. Last year, we had the opportunity to gather our current students, alumni, and faculty members to celebrate our department's 30th anniversary. We got together and looked back on all of our concerted effort and discussed what we can all do to move the department forward in the coming century.

I want to congratulate Dr. Huh once again on publishing her autobiography. Like Robert Frost's *Road Not Taken*, she'd chose the unfamiliar path in life and won unprecedented creative achievements. In moments of fear and doubt, she bravely chose the road her heart told her to and showed strength through her actions rather than words. With great love, she sowed the seeds that led to the development of Education Technology and dedicated herself in bringing about its fruits. Her passion is known not only within Korea's Education Technology field but also internationally. With her passion, she left a lasting footprint that demonstrated how education can transform individuals, corporations and people's lives.

I see her autobiography as more than a simple recording of her life. It is a historical archive of everything Dr. Huh has seen, thought and realized as she lived her life fiercely and fearlessly. It's a great book for anyone with a dream of their own, to keep and to read, especially during moments of life's tension.

Choi Yeon Mae

President of Kim Jeong Moon ALOE Co., Ltd

Everyone wants to finds happiness, and everyone wants to have people around with whom they can share their lives or who can guide us into an awakening. They can be our friends, co-workers, teachers, or mentors. Reading this book, I realized once again that having Dr. Huh's friendship is such blessing and happiness.

We all wonder once in a while what our lives would have looked like had we made a different decision at some critical point in our lives. Whenever I think about it, I ruminate over Dr. Huh's life with both envy and admiration, as if somehow it were my own un-chosen life.

We all have moments in life that deeply touch us. Recently, I visited an art exhibit called '*100 Pieces from Contemporary Korean Painting*' at MMCA (National Museum of Modern and Contemporary Art) in Deoksugung. I got to see works of masterpiece like Jung Sup Lee's *Ox* and Su Geun Park's *Wash Place*. Other touching moments in my life include watching Kyung Hwa Jung's violin performance, Gun Woo Baek's piano performance, and Su Ji Kang's ballet performance. This really speaks to the power of art and what it can provide the human spirit. These artistic masterpieces don't touch our hearts just because of their fancy techniques. I think perhaps, they touch us because the artist's soul comes through the work and touches the souls of the audience.

Right now, the Sochi Olympics are in progress, and everyone in Korea is hoping for Yu Na Kim's gold medal. When we watch her performance on ice or watch a national soccer player score a goal, we (Koreans) shout, "That was art!"

After finishing Dr. Huh's book, I couldn't help but say to myself, "That was art." Of course, no one will object to the fact that Dr. Huh's life has been like that of a beautiful white swan. After all, she has taken the most elite academic route and had quite a career, taking over pioneering projects and completing them with great enterprising success. But, it's not her academic background or her numerous accomplishments we find touching. Rather, it's the freeness of her spirit. Her book touches us because of her soul's spirit that wants to share with the world what she has learned. It is like the souls of renowned artists. The real reason her passion and accomplishments shine so brightly isn't because of her knowledge or expertise. It's because she has lived a life of sharing and giving.

It's been an incredible blessing to know Dr. Huh and a great honor to write this testimonial, but I had some concerns after I was asked. It didn't seem possible to appraise her free spirit, and I felt like all I could really say was "Wow, that is art."

Alfred North Whitehead said, "Art is born out of making patterns out of experience, and aesthetic pleasure comes from recognizing these patterns." Trying to describe this book in a few phrases would be to assess it unfairly and incorrectly, since her life is still in progress. My feelings about it should be taken as my personal aesthetic assessment of her life's experiential patterns that are described in this book.

I look forward to watching the rest of her life's journey unfold, as she lives it like a cloud that is free from any limit or space. As her name suggests, as a free-spirited citizen of the world.

Yoo Hong Joon

Former Head of the Cultural Heritage Administration,
Author of *My Essay on Cultural Heritage*

Passion That Led to the Realization of True Self

During my recent stay in Kyoto trying to write my essay on Japan, I received a text from Dr. Huh. "Professor Yoo, do you mind proofreading my autobiography?" I told her I would. Dr. Huh and I are both from the same graduating class of SNU. Though we were in different departments, we often hung out together during our theater class, working on stage props, installations and costumes. We were pretty close back then.

We both had similar personalities. too. We were outgoing, optimistic, intellectually curious and always hungry for knowledge. We would meet up after class at a café and have coffee over music, and other senior class members and friends would join us in our conversations.

We were both very competitive and combined with our thirst for knowledge, we got into a number of heated debates. We often debated over the merits of particular novels that were published in literary magazines, like *Creativity and Criticism*, a dominant authority on literature in those days. Our views sometimes led to arguments, as did our differing opinions on films. I remember one particular incident. We were talking about films, and Dr. Huh insisted that *Un Homme et Une Femme* (*A Man And A Woman*) was a great movie, while I said that *Lord Jim* was far better. At last, the argument ended with my pronouncement that we should come back to the topic after she's watched both movies again. Our friends used to laugh at us for always getting into these arguments. Looking back, I think I valued realism in art while Dr. Huh favored romanticism and pure artistic merit. These old memories make me smile and remind me of how fiery we used to be in those days.

After graduation, we went our separate ways in life and gradually saw less of each other. Then, years later, I read in a newspaper article that she had switched her major, got her PhD in the U.S. in Education Technology, and recently came back to Korea as a professor at Hanyang University. I was a little surprised but figured her passion led her to change her course. I also forecasted that with her passion, she would go on to make great social contribution in her career.

12

Then later, I was surprised once again by the news when I saw her as a parliamentarian working as a champion for the IT field. I was taken back seeing this new side of her that I'd never seen before. It felt like you could never be quite sure of the full depth she possessed. When she was appointed the president of ICU, I was working as the head of the Cultural Heritage Administration. One day, I received a call from her. "Hong Joon, I'm in Daejeon working as the president of ICU." This was the first time I had heard her voice since our graduation. Prior to that, we had met in professional settings a few times, but this was the first time I heard the voice of my friend. She had called to ask me for a favor, a speech. And on the day of the speech, we got to met for the first time in a very long time, and there, she told me about her life after college. The stories I heard that day are inside this book.

I decided to write this testimonial because having read her book, I wanted to testify to the world the one story she wouldn't or couldn't tell herself in her own autobiography. And that is the life Dr. Huh has led is the perfect example of a life that tirelessly seeks for self-realization. And I can't think it's the purity of her passion, her complete self-assurance, her bright optimism through which she looks at the world, and her unbending will I'd known since our college days are what drove her to have this life.

We can never know the exact ways in which our will is going to be manifested. However, I have faith as an old friend that whatever road she is on, it will be the best one she could have chosen in her present circumstance. One day, I might receive another unexpected message or call from her. And though I can't tell yet what she will be calling about, there's no doubt it will be another pleasant surprise, as it has always been.

Lee Sang Chul

Vice President of LG U+

When a long time friend Dr. Huh told me she'd be publishing her autobiography that will show each chapter of her life, I asked for a copy before the official release of the book. After I got the book, I read through the entire script in almost one sitting. Having studied literature once, Dr. Huh's book was filled with literary sensibilities. After finishing it, I was truly impressed and inspired.

Dr. Huh and I share a long history through the schools that we both went to. We are both alumni of the same primary school, and we also attended girls and boys' middle and high schools of the same name. Then, we met again in college and shared the campus together. Added to that, I also went to the same middle school, high school and college with her husband, Professor Jeon. Our academic ties are fundamental.

When Dr. Huh was successfully working as an IT expert at the 16th National Assembly's Science, Technology, Information, and Telecommunication Committee, I was presiding as the ceo of KT. At that time, she helped me grow the company in many ways. One day, the two of us were talking, and she told me, "I don't think it's normal that a corporation of KT's size doesn't have a single woman in its upper management. We need to promote more women to be included in these positions and raise women's status in society."

Mysteriously, even in her 60's, Dr. Huh possesses so much energy and is just as active, passionate and beautiful as she was in the earlier decades. We share a connection based on comradery which goes beyond a simple friendship. Even though she's changed her profession several times, going from a professor to a member of the National Assembly, to the head of a university, she's always focused her efforts on developing the top IT talents and marketing Korea's IT industry internationally. She conducted global diplomacy while establishing Korea's IT field. Over the years, her global orientation has gotten even stronger, and she now contributes heavily in marketing Songdo to the world and training young students.

Because we have this shared involvement in the IT industry, I can easily relate to a lot of what is written in this book. The days when she fought fearlessly for the growth of Korea's IT industry reminds me of my own efforts as well. However, her book is about so much more than her contribution to this specific field. It is indeed a wonderful stage play encapsulating the blood, sweat and tears of Dr. Huh-a woman who went abroad to study alone at a time when it was extremely rare and difficult. And upon returning, she dedicated her passion and talent for the good of her country regardless of where she was. For this reason, it is a must-read for any woman, especially for those who wish to achieve self-realization through their own chosen profession.

Jin Dae Jae

Chairman of Skylake Incuvest & Co.,
Former Minister of Information and Communication

When Dr. Huh told me she was be writing an autobiography, I was excited because I knew it would be a great book worthy of attention. I am very happy to write this testimonial because I think Dr. Huh embodies many admirable qualities that everyone could learn from, such as her bottomless passion and her consideration for others. I first met her at the Science, Technology, Information and Telecommunication Committee at Korean National Assembly. Unlike other the assembly members who can be quite harsh and blunt in their criticism of ministers, I was surprised and touched by her calmness when she spoke about policies and presented alternative ideas. I was also touched by passion when she was working to further the progress of Korea's IT industry, as the president of ICU recruiting students from developing countries and training them while she was at ICU. Though I've had many opportunities to meet her, they were mostly in formal settings on TV talk show programs. Reading her book gave me a deeper and more personal understanding of her struggles and choices, her challenges and beliefs. I think her autobiography can give people hope and empower all of us as we seek to live each day with meaning.

Dr. Huh's life is like a drama full of ups and downs, twists and turns. While reading my beloved professor's book, I wondered what my life would have been like had I never met her. After I joined the Education Technology department after much meandering, it was Professor Huh who offered me her support and understanding throughout my trials. She was a great mentor and guided me into a larger sea of knowledge and study. Professor Huh is also my life's savior who helped me become a professor at my own alma mater. To me, she will always be a mentor who demonstrated what a teacher's love for her student can be.

Professor Huh was never just a preacher. She lived by her own words and took decisive action at each critical moment of her life. This book recounts the footsteps of her personal history. At times, reading this book made me feel solemn, giving me an opportunity for deep self-reflection. There are many virtues that are needed in life, and I am truly touched by the extraordinary love and passion she has for all people and life. To have success in life, it's required for us to have profound love and passion for our own lives as well as for the people who are in our lives. It is with this kind of love she created her extraordinary life that's enclosed in this book. I think this book can be a guiding compass for anyone who wishes to pave their own unique path in life. It will also serve as a beacon of hope for those who are lost in a period of life's darkness at this moment in their life.

Kim Sung Jin
CEO of I-KAIST

Out of her book, I consider acts six and eight to be mandatory readings for all young entrepreneurs. The pure determination Dr. Huh showed while withstanding the external pressures and standing by her conviction to salvage ICU until she resigned as the president reminds us of the Indian spirit.

It is said that the Indians held a ritual praying for rain during the times of drought. They practiced the ritual because it always brought them rain afterwards. Modern scientists who researched the correlation between the rituals and the rainfall discovered that the Indians had simply performed the ritual until it finally rained. This illustrates we can achieve our heart's desires by refusing to give up. I am certain that the perseverance demonstrated in the Act 6 enabled what followed later in Act 8.

Dr. Huh's enduring nature led her to the path of public service, advocating for Education Technology, and recently, it has also led her to become one of the most powerful proponents and promoters of Start-up companies. I want to reiterate that this perseverance, the refusal to give up is the most important quality our young entrepreneurs should possess. And if you are curious about the secret to having such tenacity, the answer lies in keeping an open mind and an attitude of inclusion and acceptance.

As we see in Act 6, Dr. Huh resigned from her position at ICU, and ICU was eventually merged with KAIST. Coincidentally, I am an alumni of KAIST and currently, I am a ceo at one of its affiliated companies. Naturally, I suspected Dr. Huh might be harboring some ill feelings towards KAIST. But after meeting her, all of my suspicions were proven wrong. Even though she was adamant about her position and fought to defend it until the end, she had fully accepted the result and even gave me words of encouragement in being a young entrepreneur. My experience of meeting her is a great example which shows her life philosophy. Further proof the that my testimonial is actually included in this book!

This book narrates the life of a Korean woman who lived her life with a spirit of openness and acceptance, and I recommend this book to everyone who wishes they had more tenacity and will.

Dick Warmington

Ex-President of Samsung HP Korea and Chadwick International School

In January 2010, I was asked by my high school in Los Angeles if I would be interested in leading the founding of Chadwick School in Incheon. The school needed someone with my background. I had graduated from Chadwick in 1960 before attending Stanford University. Then later, from 1988-1992; I helped establish Samsung Hewlett-Packard (SHP) in Seoul as the president. I had been very active on two independent school boards in Northern California over the previous 10 years.

Of course, success in starting the school was heavily dependent upon my finding strong local leaders to assist me in finding the right management talent for the school. I immediately contacted two of my close friends from my earlier days running SHP. One of that was Huh Unna. To my great surprise, Unna responded that she would be interested in joining me in founding the school. I knew then that we could achieve great success in this difficult task.

Without Unna's dedicated effort in so many different ways, we would have never been able to open the school in the fall of 2010. The license to operate the school was *VERY* difficult to obtain, and there were financial issues that needed to be resolved between Chadwick and NSIC, the founder of Songdo city where the school was located, and MEST, the Korean Ministry of Education, Science and Technology.

Based on my life experiences, Unna is a one of the most talented, dedicated, creative and action-oriented people I have ever met. As a female, she had many barriers to overcome (as I learned in my experience in managing SHP) in order to accomplish all that she has. I love her description in the title of her book 'Free as Clouds, Fierce as Flame' as it characterizes her perfectly. All of what she has accomplished, as she describes in her book, would generally be the summary of accomplishments of a *dozen* high performing individuals. Also, her accomplishments span across a number of different areas in life. What an amazing woman she is!

I am so fortunate that Unna came into our family's life back in the 1990. We treasure the on-going relationship with her. It will be interesting to see what the next Act in her life will be. Whatever it is it will be amazing!

Shelly Wille

Head of School at Chadwick International School

Dr. Huh Unna has been an amazing support to the entire Chadwick International community. Her deep knowledge of education, Korean politics and history give us the connections and perspective that have been incredibly useful as we forge this new ground of international education. Unna's commitment to best practice and her true desire to continue about learning make her a wonderful support and a mentor. She is enthusiastic about new learning opportunities the International Bacclaureate and design thinking give to our students. Together, we have worked to deepen the connections to local schools and provide additional learning opportunities for our Korean and international colleagues. She is an advocate for students and teachers and a role model for our students.

Prologue

"You are destined to live like a nomad because your name has the Chinese character representing the cloud. You also resemble the souring cloud. The souring cloud is normally soft and beautiful. It seems at peace, but it can emit the highest bolt of energy when the cold and warm currents meet. All this means that you possess both great peace and energy within you." When a German friend of mine who was very curious about Eastern culture and philosophy paid a visit to a fortuneteller, this was what I received as the interpretation of my name. Perhaps, this prediction was correct. I have lived my life traveling all over the world and always staying busy. The other character 'Na' which could mean 'Jina' in Chinese, is a name our ancestors thought belonged to the biggest continent in the world. Maybe I was named this so I could travel freely like the clouds over the biggest continents in the world.

When I was in kindergarten, my parents left the city to carry on their business in the suburbs, and I was left to be raised by my strict grandmother. My childhood years were desperately lonely. My grandmother's wishes were for me to go to Seoul National University, SNU, and become an English professor. Over time, her wishes became mine as well. But after

I went to the U.S., I ended up getting my masters degree in Library and Information Science and my PhD in Educational Technology. Right before I left, one of my veteran professors said, "There is no use studying the literature of a foreign country. A new era is approaching, and what will matter is technology."

His advice really hit home with me. Thanks to his foresight, this conversation defined a decisive turning point.

As I worked on my masters and doctorate, I met my husband and gave birth to my children. I worked for a while at Florida State University where I got my PhD, but soon we had to move because of my husband's new job in Washington D.C. . After we moved to Washington D.C., I worked as an Educational Technology consultant for the American government, businesses and the army until my husband got a job offer to teach at SNU, and we decided to move back to Seoul. For a brief while, I worked at Korea Education Development Institute until I became a professor myself at Hanyang University. There, I established the first Educational Technology department in Korea. Over the years, I engaged many students while working on many projects for the Korean government, businesses and the army. Thankfully along the way, I have gained a nickname and a reputation as the 'godmother of Educational Technology.'

During the Kim Dae Jung administration, I was selected as a member of the National Assembly and got to contribute to the growth of the IT industry in Korea. In 2002, I successfully implemented the 'electronic voting system' for the first time during the presidential election, introducing the future possibility of an 'electronic democracy.'

At the following 16th presidential election, I helped mobilize the use of internet and mobile IT technology in the forefront, leading the 'cyber voting movement' which ultimately led President Roh to become the first 'Internet president.' After I finished my term at the National Assembly, I worked for four years as the president of ICU, focusing mostly on the school's specialization and globalization. After the government merged ICU with KAIST for politial reasons, I decided to resign from my post and lived a jobless, free life for two years. Then in 2010, my friendship with a long time friend led me to my current job at Chadwick as the senior advisor. Since then I've been pouring my heart and soul to promote the school and the city of Incheon as an emerging international city.

I am generally a fast person. I tend to talk, walk and act fast. But when I took a moment to stop and look back on my life that's cruised by me, I suddenly remembered Shakespeare metaphor of our lives as a play. As I recounted my past, I realized my life as a drama had 8 acts and 23 scenes. In retrospect, my life has been a series of new trials and challenges, which I charged into without much fear. A friend of mine who had been a ceo at a global corporation once said to me, "You lived your life like a shaker, mover and a pioneer." Perhaps, I have been that person who changes and moves society. But I have been more than blessed to have met countless people who helped me along the way and gave me the strength to move forward when it was difficult for me to do so.

In each act, the people and the events that influenced me led me to the next scene. There were many times when I felt as though I had reached a dead-end, but each time I pulled myself up and started moving again towards the future. Like Robert Frost's poem *The Road Not Taken*,

Two roads diverged in a yellow wood, and
I took the one less traveled by,
And that has made all the difference.

It seems I always chose a path that no one else had taken before. Rather than sharing the old path, I preferred to create a new one and share it with others. Creating the so-called 'blue ocean' always felt more comfortable for me and gave me freedom. Because I was free to be the individual I chose to be, I didn't have to be limited to the role of a female, a wife, a mother or an employee. There were times when I had to pay the price of my own decisions and the freedom that came with it. But, my freedom was to me the most important value in life, and with it, I could grow and evolve. Perhaps, among all the inspirations I encountered on the roads not taken were the teachers who showed me the many flavors of life and taught me how to unlock the doors of the future that was magical and inconceivable.

Another thing that's guided me through my sometimes lonely journey along the unknown path is my grandmother's teachings. She always stressed to me how important it is that we live 'righteously.' She taught me to "always do my best without coveting what other people have." And lastly, my favorite Romantic poet, John Keats, with whom I was enamored throughout college also said something that I have always kept close to my heart.

> "Beauty is truth, truth beauty" — that is all
> Ye know on earth, and all ye need to know.

No matter what I did and despite the challenges I faced, I always gave it my best and did my work passionately. And I never harbored greedy desires. Once I realized something was not meant for me, I let it go and looked for and challenged myself to take on something else I could succeed at. I tried my best to live my life with beauty — without the ugliness of greed. I strove to live with humility and to be considerate of others. Even though this is just my personal history, if this book could deliver a small inspiration to the readers, I would be very happy.

Huh Unna

8Acts
23Scenes

Contents

Act 6   Working with Young Geniuses in Daejeon

Act 1

I Wish to Fly High in the Sky like the Clouds

All the world's a stage,

and all the men and women merely players.

They have their exits and their entrances.

And one man in his time plays many parts,

his acts being seven ages.

— William Shakespeare, *As You Like It*

Growing Up with Strict Upbringing

Growing Up with My Grandmother Since Kindergarten

It's only natural to see my grandmother as the starting point in my life because she raised me since I was a little girl all the way until I finished college. My grandmother always wanted me to be the number one student at school and expected me to show perfectly exemplary child behavior, and I tried really hard not to let her down. She truly believed that I was the best and the brightest granddaughter in the world and could not tolerate the smallest deviations from her perfectionist expectations. Thanks to her expectations, I grew up as an extremely cautious child. But it wasn't that she locked me up or physically restricted my freedom. She let me pursue dancing and other hobbies I enjoyed and even supported me as long as they didn't interfere with the grades I was bringing home.

My grandmother's life resembled a tragic novel from the Joseon era, and she was the tragic leading actress in this novel. She was born into a distinguished family of a district magistrate in Haeju in Hwang-hae Province of North Korea. Following the customs at the time, she had an arranged marriage to a much younger boy from another wealthy, dis-

With my grandmother at the airport
right before going to America to study abroad.

tinguished family. As it often was in those days, my grandmother had to raise her young husband while also running the household. Then one day, my grandfather, then a young man, left her and their two daughters and went to Tokyo to pursue his studies. There, he met another woman and had her as a second wife as it was not an unusual custom, but didn't have any more children with the new wife.

Many years later, my grandfather returned to Korea with his new wife, and by this time, my grandmother had moved down to Seoul and was running a guesthouse in Gyedong. The relocation was actually for her daughters' education. Under the careful calculations for her daughters' future, my grandmother only accepted the best students from Gyeong-seong Imperial University (now SNU) into her guesthouse. With them in the house, she created the most refined environment she could afford for her daughters (Of course she later scored one of those male students as her son-in-law). My grandmother's guesthouse had a record player and a telephone, both rare commodities back then, and she loved listening to classical music and engaging in deep discussions with her guest students. On the other hand, my grandfather who lived with his new wife for many years, passed away after losing all of his wealth, leaving my grandmother a widow.

In Korea, the word 'grandmother' is synonymous with the word 'merciful.' Most of the students returning to school after their vacation always recount how they spent their holidays eating delicious food made by their grandma and enjoying themselves. For me, the idea of a merciful grandmother was completely unthinkable. Quite the opposite, my grandmother was synonymous with 'strict rules.'

I didn't grow up alone. I had a security fence called my grandmother, yet she was not really a parental figure for me, and so my childhood away from my parents always felt extremely lonely. In all truthfulness, this was the only time in my life when I'd contemplated suicide because of loneliness. Thinking back, I'm surprised that I had such thoughts at a young age, but I was thoroughly miserable and alone. I often prayed at night that I would open my eyes the next morning and find that everything about my life was a nightmare, and I wouldn't feel so lonely anymore. I desperately wished that this unending loneliness was just a long nightmare that will soon pass.

"You Need to Get a 100%, Not 95"

"95%? Aren't you ashamed of yourself? How can you get such a score?"

To most people, getting a 95% on a test would be good. To my grandmother, only a 100% was acceptable. Her demand that I function like a superwoman started when I started school. Her theory was, "You can lose all the money you have, but no one can steal the knowledge inside your head." There were other philosophies belonging to my grandmother I grew up hearing repeatedly, such as, "Nothing is for free in this world," and "Your abilities and competence are your wealth."

Her views on academic excellence weren't the only ones she instilled in me. She also reminded me constantly that I must do everything the 'right way.' I needed to read books the right way, walk on the streets with the right posture and even sleep in a straight posture like an 'exemplary' student. Sometimes, while she was braiding my long back hair, I would tilt my head ever so slightly, and suddenly, she would strike down at my head with the hair comb to straighten me up. She was like the strictest headmaster at a conservative female dormitory. She also stressed behaving ethically and always told me it's wrong to "lay a finger on someone else's belongings, even if it's a piece of straw." Thanks to her strict upbringing from my earliest days, it became an automatic habit for me to establish for myself the most strict moral and academic standards, which did help me becoming a professional.

Because of the constant pressure from my grandmother, I maintained my class president title for 12 years from six years of elementary school all the way through high school. When I think back, my adolescent years were no doubt suffocating. But on the other hand, perhaps the present day me could only exist because of her influence. How many children are never allowed to even dream of having fun and forced to only focus on their studies? My grandmother once explained to me that the reason she was so strict with me was because my mother, her daughter, had asked her to look after me, and she felt deeply responsible for not letting her daughter down. Borrowing the words of the poet 'Suh Jung Joo,' "For twenty three years, four fifth of what raised me was wind" (Self Portrait), four fifth of what raised me was my grandmother, and I want to sincerely thank her. She always told me that whatever I do, I must 'try my best and then submit everything to Heaven's will'(盡人事待天命), and this became the guiding motto in my life.

In Love with Dancing

My Nickname, 'Chairman Khrushchev'

Being raised by my grandmother and her strict, military-style rules, I definitely grew up goal-oriented, independent and self-directed. I went to an elementary school which was affiliated with SNU's College of Education, and it was co-ed up to grade 5. The boys in my class would call me, Chief Khrushchev, the former Russian head of state known among Korean students at that time as a 'very scary person.' Looking back, I may have been acting like the disciplinarian that my grandmother was to me.

My grandmother loved Latin music, and whenever she was happy, she would hum along to *La Cumparsita*. She told me that she used to listen to this music with her guests. Since she had an appreciation for music, she encouraged me to pursue my own hobbies 'as long as they didn't interfere with my grades.' She even encouraged me to take dance lessons, which I later did. My grandmother also enjoyed Korean traditional opera, and whenever an opera company came to town with actors like Kim Jin Jin or Kim Gyung Su, she never missed a show. After the show, mesmerized by the dance she'd seen, she kept encouraging me to take up dancing. My grandmother loved telling me about the North Korean defector-turned-dancer Choi Seung Hui, and she would describe to me in detail her facial expressions and her captivating smile, and finally, she enrolled me at Kim Jin Gul Dance Institute. Soon, I started showing signs of talent, and eventually I got to play a leading role in a performance held at the City Performance Hall. My grandmother was so excited and coached me based on her observations from Choi's performances. However, it was never forgotten that dancing was only a hobby, and my most important responsibility was my schoolwork. After enduring the lonely and shy years of primary school under my grandmother's oppressive rules, I finally entered Gyeonggi Girls' Middle School, the most prestigious and difficult school to get into in the entire country.

Upon beginning middle school, our classroom teacher (the first classroom teacher I had at this school, whose name I could never forget because it literally was spelled 'Korean Cow') asked the class which one of us had been a class president at our primary school. Of course all hands went up. So he asked us which one of us had been a class president for two, three years and so on. The number of hands gradually became less until there were only two hands left who had been the class president for all six years. Obviously, the teacher was going to choose one of us as the class president for our class. Our teacher approached us with our hands still in the air and asked each of us, "Which school did you go to?." The other kid said, "I went to Deoksoo Elementary School." Deoksoo was a school that stood right across from my school and was a very reputable school. Then the teacher came and asked me the same question. "And you?" and I answered, "I went to the school affiliated to SNU College of Education." The teacher paused for a second and pointed at me and said, "You can be the class president." So I became the first class president in my class and was able to continue my annual tradition (apologies to my classmate Kim Ha Ju who had to concede the title to me).

Student Director of Dance Competition

My passion for dance didn't fade out in the years going on to middle school and high school. My high school had an annaul 'May Day' where each class held a dance competition. I was in charge of directing the dance performances of our entire class. Of course, all this extra responsibility didn't mean I was neglecting my studies. I tried very hard not to lose my position as the top student at my school. (how stressful!) It was extremely difficult to slack off knowing that my grandmother was always watching me vigilantly from behind. She was growing really fond of telling me, "your best bet in life is to get into SNU, get an English Literature degree and become a professor," and I didn't have the courage nor a sufficiently developed self-identity to protest this order. Hence I just resigned myself to living safely within the boundaries drawn for me, following the rules that she's laid out. I realized years later that most of the student guests at my grandmother's guesthouse were English Literature or Law students, and a lot of them did become professors. More importantly, I realized that my transition to English Literature major at SNU was influenced by the fact that my grandmother's very favorite guest student had also been an English literature major at SNU.

A Familiar Path and an Unfamiliar One

The First Taste of Freedom as a University Student

"Ok, you're a grown-up now. From now on, everything concerning your life is for you to decide, and you will have to face all the responsibilities and consequences of your decisions." Once I entered university, my grandmother's attitude completely flipped. She had finally decided to let her preciously guarded granddaughter be free. Considering the era she is from, she was definitely a woman of intellectual depth and breadth, and her thoughts reflected this.

My college years passed with me enjoying my freedom for the first time like a wild animal. Of course, I had great desire to compensate for the years spent under all the oppressive and suffocating rules, and I fulfilled them by actively pursuing a broad array of interests, such as photography, film, classical music, acting, etc. I was thirsty for everything, and I wanted to feel and discover everything that I didn't know about the world. Coincidentally, it was at the school's 'Photo Art Club' that I met my future husband.

I always had a vague notion in the back of my head that after college,

I would need to go abroad to continue my studies. I think it's because going to America to study was something that my grandmother had always wanted me to do. The question remained as to which school to apply to and what subject to study once I was there. It seemed natural that I would continue with my university major and study English literature, but things didn't exactly turn out according to this plan.

Throughout college, I was deeply immersed in literature, and with my girlish sensibilities, I always wanted to write about things. As an undergraduate, I diligently worked on my writing and submitted it to the college newspaper (SNU School Newspaper). Disappointingly, they never chose my pieces for publication. Once, in my staunch refusal to accept their 'no' as an answer, I submitted my writing to an English newspaper, again with no luck. After countless rejections, it was clear that I didn't have what it took to be a real writer. I had to accept this sober truth. I guess I lacked the literary genius that is shared among successful writers, and since being a writer was no longer an option, I had to go with what I did best, which was studying. I had to capitalize on this well-honed talent and choose the path of a scholar. "Sure, the path of a scholar isn't so bad," I told myself as I began my preparations to study abroad.

Preparing to Study Abroad in the U.S.

It was very rare at this time for a female with a bachelor's degree to go abroad to study. Back then, there were no services to offer any type of help with the preparations. It was entirely up to me to do all the research and prepare everything I needed to take this next big step.

One day during my senior year in university, I was having a chat with my professor about going abroad and asking him questions, and a retired professor named Jang Wang Rok stopped by the office. Professor Jang had taught English Literature and after listening carefully to our conversation, he said, "Even if you become an expert in English literature, it will always remain literature of a foreign country. Do you really think that you could understand their literature to the same degree that they understand their own? Times are changing. You should forget literature and study more useful skills. I heard the growing field nowadays is Library and Information Science.

At first, I didn't like this distinguished professor's advice against studying his own field, but soon, a second thought led me to conclude that his advice came from his foresight into the future and his sincere desire to help me understand how difficult it is to pursue English Literature. From that day on, I began to seriously think about what he said.

It's been 20 years since Professor Jang, one of Korea's most distinguished English Literature scholars and translators in history, has passed away. In 2004, his daughter (now deceased also but who was a professor at Sogang University then) compiled and published an essay book called *But Love Is A Thing That Lasts* to commemorate the 10th anniversary of his passing. The following line from the book touched my heart deeply.

> It is a monster who cherishes ideologies and principles. Humans must live freely, respecting their natural emotions.
> An average person who enjoys books and art and embellishes their own individuality is the best.

I reflected on his memories while also thinking about how this line seemed to be telling me to live according to my own taste and desires. And looking back on my life, I think I did live my life according to my own taste and desires as an adult.

Beginning My Studies at FSU

I finally decided to follow Professor Jang's advice and chose a field that seemed to have a more promising future. With this mindset, I began researching all possible fields, their advantages and disadvantages, and ultimately chose Library and Information Science.

Once I'd made my decision, I got busy. It turned out that studying abroad was not as simple as just my making up my mind that I was going to do it. First, I had to pass multiple tests such as TOEFL, GRE, and after passing them, I had to find schools that were willing to accept me. The change in major meant I also had to learn about computers, and on top of that, I also wanted to continue studying Japanese. I converted my four years of savings (which I had set aside for this exact purpose) into U.S. dollars, and after being advised on how expensive dental care in America was, got all my dental work done locally. I tried my best to be self-reliant with only minimum financial support from my family. At the end, the only help I got from my family was the money to buy the ticket to the U.S.

After passing all the required exams, I began looking into UC Berkeley's Library and Information Science Department. However they only offered admissions without the possibility of scholarship and this was not a viable option for me since I couldn't study abroad without scholarship assistance. Once Berkeley was out of question, I began looking at other schools. My main criterion was the likelihood of getting a scholarship. Finally, I received a letter from Florida State University telling me that my scores were good enough, and they were willing admit me on a scholarship. I promptly made my decision to move to the southernmost state in America and begin at FSU. The very first step I take in my transition from an English Literature major to a scholar in Education Technology would take place at FSU.

1   With my parents and grandparents at the graduation ceremony at SNU.
2   With my high school friends at SNU graduation.

Act 2

Receiving Professional Education in the U.S.

Tell me not, in mournful numbers.
Life is but an empty dream.
For the soul is dead that slumbers,
and things are not what they seem.

Let us, then, be up and doing.
With a heart for any fate,
still achieving, still pursuing,
learn to labor and to wait.

— Henry Wadsworth Longfellow, *A Psalm of Life*

Too Focused On Studying to Notice the Passage of Time

Culture Shock Across the Pacific

Before I officially enrolled at FSU and began my studies, I took some time to visit the school library and look around. I realized then what a small world I had been living in. I always felt proud of having graduated from the finest university in Korea, but the vastness of FSU's library and all of the books that filled its shelves shocked me. The library's magnitude was simply incomparable to what we had at SNU. Not only were there many more books, FSU's library also had video files and even offered different computer services.

I suddenly recalled the time when I was writing my undergraduate thesis at SNU. My thesis was on *William Faulkner's Sound and Fury*, and I decided to go to the library to look for some books about the topic. Only, I found out quickly our library only had seven English books on the subject, and all of them were already checked out. When I went to the librarian and explained that I needed some reference books on *Faulkner*, I was told I had to wait until the books were returned. After waiting an entire month, I was finally able to get one pocket-sized book and another one shortly after that. After rummaging through these two little books, I was barely prepared to write an underwhelming thesis. This was the reality of SNU's library back in those days.

In the U.S., I noticed there was a world of difference compared to Korea even in their approach to studying. At SNU, in a class on Shakespeare, which was for all English majors, students would spend the entire semester reading just one single play, such as *Hamlet* or *Othello* from its beginning to end. In the States, students studying *Hamlet* would be required to read several related books for reference along with the actual play and also watch two to three different films to inform them about the old English style of dress, architecture and language. American classes also had much more active class discussions about these films and the acting styles of different actors. It seemed American education far surpassed Korean education in terms of instructional quality and also in sheer quantity of information. I remember being awed at watching American students learn in such a dynamic learning environment.

Losing Sleep for My Studies

Understandably, the number one obstacle I faced in the beginning of my graduate studies was the language barrier. There is a joke in Korea that whenever an American guest visits a Korean school, the English teacher is the first one to try to escape the scene. The joke is making fun of the inefficiency in English education in Korea, and how it fails to prepare our students to have a conversation with a native speaker. Not an absolute exception to this rule, I also found it difficult to understand my professors and classmates who all seemed to speak too fast for my ears to catch what they were saying. It was especially frustrating to sit in my Mass Media class, where often times we would listen to the TV news or comedy programs that dealt with social and cultural issues in America. Being completely new to these topics, I was usually the only one in class who didn't laugh at some joke everyone else understood. I realized years later that we were discussing a quote by a very famous American comedian. Although I was able to get over my insecurity about my English eventually, in the beginning, it was definitely a major problem. On top of that, there were so many books (in English!) we had to read just to keep up with the class, and I never though there was enough time to do everything. I was also working part time at the library as part of the conditions for getting the scholarship, so my time was divided even more. There was no other way to handle this problem other than to eliminate sleep.

At the time, I was getting a lot of help from other students around me. I would ask to borrow notes from my dorm roommates and asked for their help with the questions I didn't understand. I can't forget how friendly and genuinely willing they were to help me. It was an experience that taught me an important truth in life, that nobody can make it or become successful all alone.

After I got a hang of things with my school work, I finally had some time to relax, so I participated in different school festivals and even attended an event held by the Korean Student Association in Tallahassee. One year, there was an International Student Fair on campus. The event is one of my most fond memories where I wore the Korean traditional Hanbok that my grandmother had bought me and showed off my Korean fan dance.

Perhaps impressed by my dance moves, one of the local daily news-paper called *Tallahassee Democrat* published a front-page article with my picture in it. Looking back, I guess you can say I was an ambassador introducing Korean dance to the American students.

Even though I started out feeling like a fish from a small pond and there were many difficulties adjusting to the new world, I did my best and stayed focused on my studies. Thankfully, with my own effort and with the help from many generous people around me, I managed to finish my master's degree in one year. Around the time of my graduation, Dr. Lee Young Duck visited Florida, and my life plans were re-adjusted once again.

Un Na Huh of Korea Will Model Native Dress at Food Fair
... International Club to host week of festivities at FSU

A photo of me that was published with the article on *Tallahassee Democrat*, a local daily newspaper.

Changing My Path to
Educational Technology

Start-Up Founder: Educational Reformer Dr. Morgan

I have to tell the story of my teacher Dr. Morgan(1930~2009) to whom fate had introduced me.

Dr. Robert M. Morgan was a Korean War veteran with a PhD in Education from Ohio State University. He went on to teach at University of New Mexico, and while he was there, he co-founded a 'general program teaching method company' and served as its president. Later, he also served as the director at a large-scale defense company called 'Litton Industries' and worked in the FBI under the U.S. Department of Education. Then, in 1968, he began his newly appointed post as a professor at FSU and the head of its Department of Education. At FSU, he played a crucial role in establishing the LSI (Learning System Institute). Dr. Morgan was a founder of a Start-up company and an education reformer at the same time, and he received sizable research funding from USAID, an agency which managed foreign aid. Soon thereafter, the Korean government invited him to take over the Sector Analysis enterprise part of its Five Year Economic Plan. When he arrived, he strongly suggested the Korean government build a specialized organization for its Education, and KEDI (Korea Education Development Institute) was built as a result. Since then, KEDI has restructured Korea's educational system and helped Korea become a country with a powerful educational system. During this time, Dr. Morgan chose Dr. Lee as KEDI's director.

The Fateful Encounter with My Life's Teacher Dr. Morgan

After establishing KEDI, Dr. Lee sent a large number of its researchers to FSU to receive their masters and PhD's. It was around this time that Dr. Lee decided to pay a visit to FSU where so many KEDI employees were studying. Since he wanted to meet with the Korean students during his visit, we students organized a small meeting and invited Dr. Lee. At the meeting, all the students shared their experiences of studying abroad, and when my turn came, I told him, "As a student studying Library and Information Science, I can't help being shocked by how advanced their library system is. The U.S. is already using the Online Computer Library Catalog (OCLC) system. This is a database used by librarians to track where all the books are located. With this system, when libraries pass books from one another, it automatically shows who has which books. For example, if a student wants to look into a very specific topic within a particular subject and asks a librarian for reference materials, he or she can use OCLC and let the student know where they are. They can tell the student a book's specific location at a university or a library. The OCLC provides data over long distances. I think Korea really needs to introduce these kinds of advanced systems, so I'm going to go into this area for my doctorate. After I'm finished with my degree, I plan on returning to Korea to introduce the system to Korean libraries."

After hearing me, Dr. Lee said, "You know, I think you're rushing this, trying to give butter to people who are still eating bean paste. You might be in over your head." I was taken back by his reaction. His response was an unexpected one, and I thought to myself, "If the director of KEDI has such thoughts about reforming the Korean library system, any attempt at innovation will be ineffective if I approach it as a library specialist. To change libraries, I'll need to become a decision maker at a higher level, at the level of education in general. Maybe if I change my focus to Education, I'll be able to reform Korean libraries from the bigger framework of advancing the education in Korea."

A few days after I got these whims in my head, I had a chance to see Dr. Morgan and tell him about the discussion I had with Dr. Lee. I also told him about the idea that I had following our discussion. Then surprisingly, Dr. Morgan began encouraging my ideas. He told me, "Yes, Unna, you should come under my instruction and pursue your PhD in Education Technology." I ended up agreeing with him, and this is how our life-long bond began. I had been heading towards Library Informatics until then. However, meeting Dr. Lee modified my direction, and Dr. Morgan finally redirected me to Education Technology. Dr. Lee had opened my first curtain to Education Technology.

Savior of Korea's Education

The three elements Education Technology are Education Psychology, Communication and Management. Management is about understanding the big picture before attempting to build the educational system in a systematic manner. For instance, after receiving a request to help build a country's educational system, we would first need to look at the bigger questions, such as "What are the country's larger goals in contrast to where it is at now" and "What do its people want to create?" From there, we try to figure out what capabilities are needed to make this happen. The final educational system would be built around these goals. Planning this way is the best way to ensure that a country evolves systems that will fit with its current state and its future goals.

Dr. Morgan made great contributions to building the Korean educational system, and they should be noted with deep appreciation in the history of our education. During his work at KEDI, he analyzed the current Korean education, introduced the mastery learning model, developed a new elementary educational process and advocated for new ways of teaching, such as incorporating the educational TV programs.

Following *Plato*'s words, Dr. Morgan lived by his belief that '*human beings could only become truly human through education.*' During the many projects he pursued with developing countries, he always preached and acted on his belief that what people needed more than bread was '*freedom from ignorance.*' He truly believed that all of society's evils, including poverty and illness, came from ignorance. He was extremely dedicated to building educational systems in developing countries and he exemplified a true educator to me.

Gaining International Project Experience

The majority of my PhD work consisted of helping Dr. Morgan with his research projects as his teaching assistant. Being his TA meant being involved in education development projects with countries like India, Indonesia, Columbia, and a number of African countries. These experiences gave me a global view and were foundational for the numerous global projects I initiated later on.

When we build an education system in a developing country, the system needs to reflect the country's current state. For instance, in South American countries where the literacy rate is high, we will teach them to create 'village newspaper' so people can read it and see the value of knowledge. This process is usually facilitated by the people in the village with some level of formal education. Once the paper is made, we would gather the village women and have them read the paper aloud by the well. This process can then help people become more conscious of what's going on around them. Similar strategies have been used with a 'village radio' to bring the local people to greater enlightened state about the world. A farmer coming home after a day's work could turn on the radio and listen to the village news and other educational lectures that were created as part of the continuing education program for the public. Another important component is building libraries throughout the entire country. For those who are illiterate, the libraries near the well or village centers would have librarians to answer their questions. The librarian would also be responsible for finding and explaining the information requested by the villager.

While I was working on my PhD, my husband had finished his army services and joined me at FSU to begin his masters degree. Just as I was finishing up my doctorate, my husband began his masters.

Soldiers at Fort Benning and a Pregnant Asian Lady

As I was preparing for my doctoral thesis, our department received an enormous research grant of 5 million dollars from the Defense Department. The U.S. Department of Defense invests a lot of money supporting the research and development in cutting edge technologies. It's well-known that engineering technologies like artificial intelligence all came from the American military. The U.S. also sends its soldiers to universities all around the country to study and participate in research and financially supports university research projects. The 5 million dollars we received came with the request that we apply the latest information technology in education to help increase the quality of military training and education. In other words, they wanted us to build a system that would enable every soldier to get their training using a computer. Later, FSU did build exactly that kind of system (called Computer Based Training or CBT) within the larger paradigm of IPISD (Inter Procedure Instructional System Design). Since I was personally involved in this project, my doctoral thesis topic was unprecedented. I chose to write about the application of IPISD in the

American military training.

Fort Benning is situated in the outskirts of Columbus in Georgia and is called the 'hometown' of the American army. This base had training facilities for new soldiers, tactical schools, a school for infantry and other educational facilities. They also housed a number of special forces and combat units. The entire facility was home to 120,000 stationed personnel, which was larger than Korea's Training and Doctrine command center, Nonsan Army Training center and several other combat units combined.

I was part of the program that developed and taught soldiers at Fort Benning how to use the new M203 Grenade Launcher. This model was used as an attachment to the M16 rifle and M4 carbine.

When I left for Fort Benning, I was seven months into my pregnancy. One December day in 1975, I drove four hours from Florida to Georgia with my stomach completely full with my unborn baby. For the next several weeks, I taught soldiers how to use the weapons system programs I developed using videos and simulations. The training consisted of teaching the soldiers how to disassemble, clean, re-assemble and combine the M203 with other weapons. As it was the very first training program that was based on our ISD (Instructional Systems Design) mode, we were anxious to see the results. American soldiers, as it turned out, were not as disciplined as their Korean counterparts. I'm thankful that this group of soldiers who could be somewhat difficult to control was surprisingly receptive to the instructions of a pregnant Asian lady and actively participated in the experiment.

Military training is fundamentally different from the run of the mill social education. For instance, in everyday education, a student could pass a course with the score of 80 percent out of a 100. But in military training, you have to get the perfect score to pass. The reason is obvious. In military, if a someone doesn't know what they're doing perfectly, it could jeopardize everyone else on the combat field. Luckily, the soldiers who received their training from me all graduated with perfect scores.

The results of my experiment at Fort Benning were phenomenal. The military was delighted that computer-based training slashed training time by a third of what it had been. Since time equals money, they got to save a third of their budget. In practical terms, the new system also saved the military a lot of building space needed to store all the required books. One new educational system had successfully brought about superior training results and revolutionary cuts in training budget, time and space. My doctoral thesis ended on this celebratory note, and in January 1976, I achieved my first life goal of getting my PhD. Coincidentally, I was the youngest among all the students studying in the U.S. to have done so. I began to imagine new dreams about returning to Korea, starting my own global projects, and becoming a true educator like my mentor Dr. Morgan.

Getting Married and
Giving Birth Abroad

Getting Married in the U.S.

I'd grown up alone with my grandmother and after moving to America, I again lived alone while trying to manage my busy schedule. After my husband finished his first semester, we finally had our wedding. I barely knew the meaning of a marriage. Everything had to be rushed because FSU only gave us three weeks for our winter vacation, and there was a lot to plan. We told our parents in Korea that we were going to have our wedding here, then started looking for a wedding hall. Our wedding took place in a Presbyterian church in Tallahassee. My husband was Catholic and wanted our wedding to be Catholic, but we were told that a Catholic style wedding would take three weeks to prepare, so we decided to go with the other church and have a very small intimate wedding.

My parents had known about their future son-in-law for a while. They had met him at the airport the day I left Korea when everyone had come to say good-bye. When we told our parents we were getting married in America, our parents said they would have another small ceremony for us in Korea. At my wedding in Tallahassee, Dr. Morgan walked me down the aisle instead of my father.

Receiving My PhD and Giving Birth

After we got married, we moved to a two-story alumni apartment building. It was a beautiful apartment complex surrounded by a lake and grassy fields where I raised my first child, my son.

While I was pregnant with my son, I continued to work on my thesis. The thesis required a lot of editing and took ten revisions. With all that typing on an old type writer, it must have been quite noisy for my son in my belly the whole time. On the day I finished the last part of the degree process, the oral exam, Dr. Morgan jokingly said, "Congratulations Unna, two PhD's are born today." He was giving credit to my son who had to endure the incessant typing noise I made.

Somehow, my giving birth to my son at the Tallahassee Memorial Hospital appeared on the local newspaper. I even got some Korean-style seaweed soup (traditionally eaten by Korean women right after giving birth to replenish energy) and dumplings from a local Korean businessman and his wife who had read the article. I was so hungry because the hospital's policy was to put the mothers on a special diet right after the baby was born, the total opposite from what happens in Korea. I remember I hid the food from the doctors and ate it when no one was around. Of course, since I had no idea what marriage was about, I also had no clue what motherhood was about either. I bought a copy of Dr. Spock's book on *childrearing* and used it as my guide in raising my son. The book gave suggestions like, "Right after the baby has gone potty, bring the baby to the sink immediately and wash, dry and powder." I used to work on the first floor while the baby was sleeping on the second floor, and I would have to run upstairs in the middle of doing my work every time the baby woke up. Every day, I climbed up and down the stairs so many times. Thanks to all that exercise during this time, I was in the best shape ever.

1 Dr. Morgan walking me down the aisle in my father's place.
2 One of our wedding photos taken in Tallahassee.

One thing Dr. Spock emphasized was the importance of breastfeeding. And being a faithful student, I stuck to this rule diligently. When I went back to work after three months, I even bottled my breastmilk and had the baby-sitter feed it to my son.

From a Professor to a Consultant

Dr. Morgan's Advice to Me, "Don't Worry, Be Happy"

After I received my official PhD, I went from being a student to being a research professor. This meant that I was no longer Dr. Morgan's student but his colleague, albeit one that was far junior to him.

After I became a professor, Dr. Morgan assigned me my own office. At that time, there was a world-renowned visiting professor at FSU named Dr. Gagné who was absent on international trips, and Dr. Morgan told me I could use Dr. Gagné's office. I was lucky to start my new job in one of the best offices.

Now that I was a professor, I had to choose my teaching assistants and carry out my own projects. This I did successfully by giving full encouragement to my students. One of the principles I always stressed to my students was 'meeting the deadline,' and I constantly reminded my students to finish their work on time.

One day, one of my graduate students from Ghana named Koonlie came to talk to me about a project. He was a bit slow-paced and laid back, which was the complete opposite of me, and secretly, I was always disapproving of this tendancy of his. One time, I showed my discontent and raised my voice at him for not doing his work and seeming unconcerned. His face turned pale. He turned to me and said, "You're a slave driver!" His words astonished me. He thought I was overseeing his work as if he was a slave.

When I was a PhD student, Dr. Morgan would catch me feeling anxious or worried, and he would always say to me, "Don't worry Unna, just be yourself. Take it easy and be happy." And every time he told me that, I'd say to myself, "How can I not worry when there is so much work to do? How can I *take it easy*?'" Decades later, I find myself giving the exact same advice to my lower-classmen and younger colleagues.

After Koonlie left my room, I ran to Dr. Morgan's office and told him "Dr. Morgan, Koonlie just called me a 'slave-driver'." Dr. Morgan just smiled and said, "Unna, you can't expect everyone else to live up to your expectations. Besides, your expectations are too high. No one can live up to them."

Since then, I have always remembered his words, and it's become a guiding principle when dealing with other people, especially people who work for me. I remember a female teaching assistant I had at Hanyang University. She was very sweet and feminine and by anyone's standard a very lovely student. But just like Koonlie, she liked to take her time with her work and took the more relaxed approach, which often got on my nerves. Sometimes our projects would get delayed because of this, and I wanted to take her aside and scold her. But I remembered Dr. Morgan's words and held myself back. Similar incidences continue to happen in my life even now, and sometimes I do let out some steam, but I mostly try my best to see things from their perspective instead of imposing my own on them.

Getting the 'Distinguished Alumni Award' at FSU.

Receiving the 'Distinguished Alumni Award' from FSU

After working as a professor for two years, I followed my husband to Washington D.C. . Before I left, my school was kind enough to put a photo of me and Dr. Gagne on the lobby wall of Dodd Hall. Korean collegues and students who visited FSU later have told me that whenever they went there, people from the school would ask them if they knew me. Then, in 1989, I received the 'Distinguished Alumni Award' from FSU. Out of many awards I've received in my life, this one really meant a lot to me. It was great being recognized by my alma mater.

Leaving the Ivory Tower Behind to Enter the War Zone

While I was working as a professor, my husband got his PhD in Statistics from FSU. As soon as he got his degree, a teaching opportunity presented itself at University of Maryland, which was close to Washington D.C. . My husband was anxious to get the job and suggested that we moved out there. I went to see Dr. Morgan for career advice and what to do about this situation. He listened and said, "Unna, there are many consulting firms catering to public officials who work for the federal government. Many are looking for education technology specialists to come work as consult-ants. I will write you a recommendation for a company I know."

The company he introduced me to was called *Athena*. As soon as we arrived in Washington D.C., I went there and met with its head, Judy Springer. When I handed her the recommendation letter, she said, "Oh, it's from Dr. Morgan." There was a brief interview, and right away, I was told that I could 'start work tomorrow.' I had passed the interview. I realized then just how powerful Dr. Morgan's letter was. Since then, it's not been lost on me just how important a reference from an influential figure is in American society, and I would gladly to write one for all of my students. One of my students, Yoo Young Man, who's now a professor at Hanyang, came to ask me for a letter when I was a professor. He came from an engineering background and had been working for Korean Electric Power Corporation before coming to the college. I remember sympathizing with him because he came from a different background than my other students, had financial challenges and seemed lonely. Because I knew he was very mature and diligent, I asked Dr. Morgan if he could help him out. I told him about Young Man's difficulties and asked if he could offer him full scholarship at FSU. Dr. Morgan agreed. Thanks to his generosity, Young Man was able to finish his PhD at FSU without any more financial burden. After his studies, I also helped him by referring him to Samsung Human Resources Development Center, where I was working on a project at the time. It felt good to return the care and love I'd received from Dr. Morgan to my own student.

Giving Education Consultation to Global Corporation AT&T

Until this point, I had lived in a protected ivory tower of a university campus as a student or a professor. Most people I'd met at school had outstanding character and were intellectually inclined. In other words, the university environment where I'd spent most of my professional life was very much a fenced area separate from the real world. Unlike there, the consulting field was governed by the principle of '*survival of the fittest*' and resembled a jungle. Consulting companies make money by giving professional advice to their clients. If the advice produces results that make the clients happy, they receive a big paycheck. If the client is not satisfied, the consultant is fired. This was my world now.

The first client I took on at Athena was a global company AT&T, which possessed the famous *Bell Laboratories*. At the time, AT&T had 14,000 employees globally, and they were leading the world in communications and specializing in long-distance phone calls. They wanted to expand their business from the current communication territory to communication and computer territory and solidify their brand identity and get rid of the bureaucratic corporate culture. In short, they were looking to reinvent themselves so they could remain effective and competitive in the future computer era. To do this, AT&T implemented corporate restructuring and divided itself into eight parts. Also, they were looking for a new educational program to prepare their employees to meet these new challenges, and I was going to be a part of this project.

We began by following our usual protocol. First, we tried to understand exactly what AT&T wanted. I interviewed countless employees all the way to its ceo to figure out what the company truly needed. From this, it became clear that the company needed to be functioning more effectively and also the workers had to be working at a higher level. Next, I came up with a very detailed education program based on my analysis of the company mission and vision and set goals and strategies to achieve them. One of the things I learned from the interview was that between the upper management and the rest of the employees, there was a big difference in what people thought was the company's vision and its time frame. Leaders tended to look ten or so years further ahead into the future and had a larger vision for the company than the regular employees.

Taking Countless Flights

I applied everything I'd learned at FSU in carrying out my project. Sometimes I was working on three to four projects simultaneously which really pushed me to utilize my full potential. As I was taking on so much work, some people within the company started saying that I operated on 'horsepower' while others became envious. I didn't really pay attention to what was being said about me and only focused on my work and producing results. Then once I'd produced satisfactory results, I asked for a raise. Within one year, I had managed to receive three raises from Athena. In 1978, the starting salary for a professor in Washington D.C.

was around 12,000 dollars. My starting salary at Athena was higher, and by the end of the second year, I was making three times more than a university professor.

AT&T had eight divisions including *Eastern Bell* and *Southern Bell*, and they had a headquarter in each region. I traveled around to each regional office and gave educational consultation to their management. I was on countless flights back then, and eventually, I realized the Chinese letter for 'cloud'(雲) in my name must have hinted at this lifestyle. During this time, I saw so many clouds through the airplanes windows.

The Swan Pedals Ceaselessly under the Water

Even though talking in front of a room full of AT&T managers was called a 'lecture,' in reality, it was closer to going to a battle. The management often consisted of people in their 40's and 50's with a lot of seniority and experience. They didn't feel like there was anything new to learn about the company they'd been working at for so long. On the other side, I was a young and relatively inexperienced professional in her 20's trying to teach them something new because I had a degree from Education Technology. Some of my audience had an overtly racist attitude towards me, clearly offended at the idea of being 'taught' by a woman of color. Others subjected me to mental torture by asking the most absurd questions during the Q&A sessions. I usually dressed in a professional suit and put on a dignified smile. However, I was always anxious and unsure if people were really satisfied with my lecture. I worried whether the audience could fully understand my English, and if anything I'd said was helpful at all to them. Sure, I was smiling on the outside and, I might have seemed graceful, like a pretty swan floating on a lake. But like the swan, I was pedaling for my dear life to stay afloat. After spending all my energy at work, my body felt so heavy like a stack of wet cotton by the time I got home. Sometimes, living this life would bring me to tears when I was alone.

Subject of Envy of All My Colleagues

Soon, something was starting to get stirred up in the company about me among my colleagues. As words spread about this 'horsepower' like energy and pace at which I was working, other clients started coming to me and offer me to work on their next project. When this started happening, some of my colleagues started to get envious. Some people couldn't stomach the fact that a bulk of the company's work was now being sent to me. No one was outwardly rude to me, but I would hear people whisper about me in the corners, and it wasn't pleasant to walk around the company.

There was one particularly beautiful female colleague, who was having an affair with a senator at the time. She used to come to me saying, "Are you trying to bury yourself in work?" She tried to get me to slow down by talking about her fun colorful life in Washington D.C. (which I understood only after getting into politics myself much later). Another young secretary working for the ceo was blatantly racist towards me and made my life difficult especially when I needed her administrative help.

Getting Scouted by Another Company

As I continued to work hard, I got a job offer from another consulting company. They offered me a salary that was twice what I was making then. I felt a little guilty as if leaving the job was a kind of betrayal to Judy, but finally, I decided to take the offer. Then, one month into the new job, my husband and I had to move back to Korea.

When I was working as a consultant, I had also the opportunities to work with many other major corporations, such as *Pratt & Whitney*, which specializes in airplane engines, *Citibank* and the *U.S. Department of Housing and Urban Development*. It was a ruthless job where the only thing that mattered was your performance. My experience as a consultant really paved the way for the projects I did later with Korean businesses. I had developed enough fighting strength to face the future challenges in Korea.

KBS Chooses My Husband and Me as 'The Most Successful Koreans in America'

In February of 1981, the Korean President Jeon Doo Whan came to Washington D.C. with a team of reporters for the U.S.-Korea summit talk. One of the reporters, Mr. Kim, paid my husband and me a visit wanting to interview us for a program called '*Koreans Who Achieved the Most Success in America.*' They decided we were the right candidates because both of us had gotten our PhD degrees in America.

My husband was interviewed first on his university campus in Maryland, and I was interviewed at my Athena office in Bethesda in Washington D.C. . They also came to our apartment in the suburbs and took photos. Thanks to this, when we arrived in Korea later, several of our friends told us they had enjoyed watching us on the program. Though my parents had videotaped the whole thing, we later lost the tape, and sadly, I never got to watch it myself.

Cooking Skills I Mastered While Living Abroad

My husband enjoyed inviting other Korean students to our home, and every time he did, it was up to me to prepare a meal for them. Being my impatient self, I also took up cooking and learned it in no time. I mastered the art of preparing multiple dishes simultaneously, and later when I became a member of the assembly, I even wrote a piece called 'Cooking is Science.' To make several dishes simultaneously, you first gathered all your ingredients, slice them and put each ingredient on separate plates. Next, you cook from the order of cold dish to hot dish. So, if there were four dishes I was making for dinner, I'd make all four at once. Our stove had four stovetops, so I would have a different dish cooking on all four tops as I monitored and adjusted for heat. This way, all the dishes would be finished nearly at the same time. My husband used to brag to people, "When my wife goes into the kitchen, food comes out unusually quickly." Impatient people take care of all things quickly, and I tend to walk, talk, think and act fast.

When we were graduate students living in Tallahassee, we used to invite a lot of our American friends and serve them Korean food like Bulgogi, Kimbab and Japchae. They generally loved it and told us Korean food was the best. When I first arrived in the U.S., I didn't even know how to make Kimchi, but months went by and as we entertained more guests, my cooking skills improved a lot. During the semester off I had between my masters and PhD, I worked as a waitress at a Chinese restaurant. It was run by the wife of one of the school librarians and was a fairly well-known place in Tallahassee called *Lucy Ho*'s so I was able to make good money from my tips alone. While I was working there, I also got to learn how to make a few Chinese dishes by watching the kitchen staff. Unfortunately, serving food wasn't my strongest suit, and one time, I spilt red wine all over a customer's expensive silk shirt, causing me great embarrassment. This is another piece of memory from my time studying in America.

1 After receiving my masters degree.
2 With my friends.
3 With my advisor Dr. Morgan at my PhD ceremony.

An Opportunity to Serve in My Home Country

When you are joyous, look deep into your heart.

And you shall find it is only that

which has given you sorrow that is giving you joy.

When you are sorrowful look again in your heart,

and you shall see that in truth.

You are weeping for that which has been your delight.

— Kahlil Gibran, *The Prophet*

A New Beginning
at the Educational Development Institute

Back to Seoul with My Husband

In Korea, there is a saying that "A woman's destiny is that of a gourd," which basically means a woman's destiny is determined by the type of man she marries.

I moved to Washington D.C. from Florida because my husband was asked to teach at University of Maryland. We moved so we could both work and have two income. It was also from this move I received the opportunity work as a consultant. When we decided to come back to Korea, once again, it was for my husband's job. I guess I exemplified the old saying that wives should follow their husband's path.

While I was still working as a consultant in Washington D.C., one of the veteran Korean professors named Jung Bum Mo came there to recruit professors. At the time, Professor Jung was the head of Chungbook University, and after meeting my husband and me, he asked us to come back to Korea. Professor Jung wanted to offer both of us a position as a professor, but my husband was unsure. Back then, there weren't too many people in Korea with an American doctorate, and we had received job offers from several different universities. Each time my husband got an offer to come back, he declined. Judging by this, I thought we would be staying in America permanently, but we didn't. When he was asked in the summer of 1981 to teach at his alma mater, Seoul National University, he very eagerly accepted the offer. I had just started working at my new company for a huge salary. But as my husband had already decided we would move back, I had to leave behind the new job and the new salary and start packing my luggage. Since we didn't have a home in Korea, we decided we would stay with my parents who had just moved to Seoul from Busan.

Building My First Nest at the Korean Educational Development Institute (KEDI)

Even though my husband had a job offer lined up, all of this was sudden for me, and I did not have enough time to look for a new job before we left America. Since the previous offers I got from Korean universities were no longer valid, I had to start looking for new opportunities.

Professor Lee Young Duk, who visited FSU often due to all the researchers he sent there, had always said to me, "I will always have a position ready for you Dr. Huh. Just come to KEDI whenever you are ready." Unfortunately for me, Professor Kim was no longer working as the head of the institute when I came to Korea. Instead, there was a new professor in his place, Dr. Hong Woong Sun. Although I didn't know Dr. Hong personally, most people who had come to FSU through Dr. Lee and people I knew at FSU were working in upper management at the institute. I reached out and let them know I was returning to Korea. After settling into our new home in Seoul, I made an appointment to see Dr. Hong and say hello. When we finally met in person, Dr. Hong said to me,

"I've heard so much about you from many people. Our pervious head Dr. Lee told me you helped him a lot, and you also helped many of our students at FSU and even helped them get scholarships. We really appreciate you helping our students despite your own busy schedule. I know you've helped almost every one of our students. I even heard that you gave a student a ride from home to the airport after they finished their studies. Thanks to you, our institute was able to build very close ties to FSU."

He paid me so many compliments it made me blush. He told me I could start working right away and asked me to take on a dual role as the head of International Cooperation division and the Research section.

Busy Days Attending International Events

It seemed that wherever I went, I brought in a lot of work. As soon as I started working for the Institute, I was asked to oversee an international event celebrating the 100th year anniversary of U.S.-Korea diplomatic relations. Even though the actual anniversary date was May 22, 1982, the planning began earlier in 1981, and the 100 American editors I was welcoming arrived in Korea around the anniversary date. It was a very busy time hosting these guests, conducting seminars and introducing the guests to Korean education.

At the time, the institute was building the foundations for Korea's primary and secondary education and doing a lot of research and development. Between 1981 and 1982, the concept of mastery Learning was just being introduced to schools, and there were various studies being done on the educational value of television. Due to this, many well-known academic figures were coming to Korea to learn about Korea's educational reform. Seminars were held with guests from developing and developed countries, and after the seminar, I took the guests and gave them an educational tour of industrial cities like Pohang and Ulsan and showed them historical sites in Gyeongju.

"We Need to Pay Extra Kindness to Our Guests from Developing Countries"

Once, we had several guests from different countries coming to attend our international seminar. It was our job to pick up our guests from the airport and escort them to Seoul. Usually, we would send separate cars to pick up individual guests who arrived at different times. On this day, I realized that one of the cars going to the airport was a beat-up van. I asked who we were picking up and was told it was one of the guests from a developing country. I thought this was unconscionable and asked, "How can we send a nice SUV to guests coming from a developed country and an old van to ones from a developing country?" It seemed like a rude gesture to treat guests from countries differently. I also believed it was important to be extra kind to those coming from developing countries. We needed to make a good impression so they would keep coming back to learn from us. Upset by this discriminatory treatment, I went to speak to my boss who was in charge of planning. I asked him how this could be. We were in the hallway and our voices got higher and higher. People stopped to watch us until Dr. Hong, the president saw us and called me into his office. In his office, he asked what was going on, and I explained to him. Surprisingly, Dr. Hong simply told me that if there's ever a problem of inadequate transportation, I could always use his work car. This incident brought me and Dr. Hong closer together.

Playing Multiple Roles Is Challenging

When in Korea, Do As the Koreans Do …

After I came back to Korea, I quickly learned that the Korean culture was very different from the American one. In Korea, married working women were expected to perform their domestic responsibilities perfectly and handle their other roles simultaneously. Often, whenever I felt pressured by these expectations, I had to remind myself, "This is Korea."

I became pregnant with my second baby soon after I came back to Korea. Early into my pregnancy, I had an accident. I was walking on a very slippery hallway floor at the institute when I slipped and fell. My whole pregnant body began to ache. Since I was worried about the baby inside, I finished my work early that day and came home. Later, Dr. Hong heard about my accident and ordered a carpet to be placed in the hallway. He was worried I might fall again and lose the baby. President Hong continued to be kind to me and even sent me congratulatory flowers when I delivered my baby.

Even though Dr. Hong was looking out for me with extra kindness, my work at the institute was not easy. I always had a lot of work with my dual role and felt a lot of pressure to be an exemplary female scholar as there were only a handful of us in the academia. Some people were also envious of me and all the work I was doing, and some so especially because I was a woman.

At home, I had many mom responsibilities which weren't so easy either, and I was also experiencing culture shock while trying to adjust to a new life living with my in-laws. After living with my parents for three months, we moved into a new apartment and lived with my in-laws. However, the clincher of it all was the change I saw in my husband. Back in Washington D.C., my husband would help me with household chores, like doing the dishes and picking up our son from the daycare, and generally acting like a Western-style husband. Once we were back in Korea, he stopped doing all of this and didn't so much as glance at the piled dishes in the kitchen sink. He even added pressure by asking me to be more like a 'housewife.' He would say things like, "Yesterday, my colleague's wife packed him a lunch with bone stew, and it was so delicious." Hearing him say this made me think, "With the amount of work I have, I think I should be the one eating the nicely prepared stew." With the added pressure coming from my husband, I started becoming more and more stressed. My morning sickness grew worse, the pressure to perform at work was mounting, and at home I was expected to be the perfect daughter-in-law. Finally, I decided it was time to hire a full time help to take some of this pressure off of me.

Father-In-Law I Admire

Once when I was back in Washington D.C. working as a professor, a very gentlemanly Korean professor named Dr. Jo Sung Ok came to FSU as an exchange professor and sat in the office next to me. He had served as an Assistant Secretary for the Ministry of Education and told me he had come to FSU on the recommendation of Dr. Morgan with whom he had worked closely on Korean educational reform. Since our offices were close by, we had many chances to talk to each other, and we became close. He often came to visit our family and play with our son.

One day when we were talking together, I found out that he was an old student of my father-in-law. My father-in-law had graduated from Bosung Specialty School and became the head of Dongsung High School when he was 30. He was also a beloved student of another head of Dongsung Highschool named Jang Myun and followed his teacher's lead into becoming the head of school. Later, Mr. Jang went into politics and became Korea's prime minister, and my father-in-law did everything he could to support him. During one of our convertsations, Dr. Jo told me that the famous Korean artist Chu Dong Sung's cartoon character 'Dr. Jjang Gu' was created after my father-in-law. He told me how he grew up very privileged in an extremely affluent family. Then one day when he was the class president, he made a mistake and my father-in-law called him into his office and slapped him in his face. He told me he was surprised I was the daughter-in-law of his renowned teacher and marveled at how small the world was. He also told me about all the innovative things my father-in-law did as the school principal. Listening to him, I realized for the first time what an extraordinary man my father-in-law was.

Before coming back to Korea, I had never met my father-in-law. Hence, I was especially thoughtful when choosing a gift for him to give upon our return, and since then, my father-in-law had always taken special care of me. He became my biggest supporter, when I briefly entered in politics later. He's passed now, but as time goes by, my memory of him grows stronger and fonder.

1

2

1 President of the institute, Hong Wong Sung. The Thai minister of education and his wife.
2 Dr. Hong and other members of the Institute.
3 At the Institute (KEDI).
4 Trip to Gyeongju with our guests for the 100th year anniversary.

3

4

1

1 At an Education Technology training camp with representatives from South East Asia.
2 Me receiving a plaque of appreciation from the American editors.
3 Visiting the Pohang Steel with American editors.

2

3

Act 4

My Beautiful Connection to
Hanyang University

Some are born great

some achieve greatness

and some have greatness thrust upon them.

— William Shakespeare, *Twelfth Night*

Founding the First Educational Technology Department in Korea

Laying Down the Bridge to Hanyang University

Working at the KEDI for two years, I learned a lot about the inner realities of Korea's educational arena and received a lot of help from President Hong. However, I always kept my childhood dream of becoming a university professor which was also my grandmother's dream for me. In regards to my moving on to a university setting, Dr. Lee Young Duk recommended Seoul National University and Ewha Womans University. He strongly recommended me to go to Ewha where his wife was working. But for some reason, having only women students didn't appeal to me despite the fact that my own mother had once wanted me to go to Ehwa where she had also gone. The other option was SNU. I knew SNU wasn't going to be an easy place to find employment, but it wasn't impossible either. The drawback of SNU was there were many senior faculty members in the Education department, and as a result I could foresee a lot of hierarchical tension and conflicts associated with it. I also thought I might become a bit alienated at SNU because there were many graduates from the College of Education, and I had a liberal arts background in

English Literature. I wasn't sure I could really push forward with our new department in this environment, and in truth, the odds didn't look good. These factors combined made SNU unappealing. Then one day, Dr. Hong made me a very attractive offer. He asked me to come to his office for tea and told me; "You know before coming here, I was a professor at Yonsei University for a long time. One of my students from Yonsei is Kim Jong Yang, and he is a son of the Chairman Kim Yun Jun at Hanyang University. Jong Yang is doing his PhD right now at Columbia University in Educational Technology. I talked with his father about his future, and it seems he has little interest in coming back to Korea. This made me think of you, so I asked the chairman that since his son is in the States, why not bring Dr. Huh to Hanyang and have her found the Educational Technology department first? I told him that this way, when Jong Yang comes back, he can settle in nicely. He thought it was a great idea and agreed to bring you in. What do you think?" And this is how thankfully, Dr. Hong created the bridge for me to get to Hanyang Univerisity, and so began my long history with the university.

Six Months of Teaching Experience Lost

I decided on Hanyang University because of the connection made by Dr. Hong and Chairman Kim, but getting into its College of Education still had its ups and downs. Although it was the chairman himself who decided to hire me, I still wanted to follow the proper protocol. I took my resume and went to see the Dean of College Shin Guk Bum. I introduced myself and told him that I came to see him on the recommendation of Dr. Hong. He welcomed me and told me I could start teaching in the fall semester of 83. But there was a catch. The ranking system for professors began from assistant professor to associate to fulltime professor, and he wanted me to start from the bottom as an assistant professor ignoring my previous experience since getting my PhD. I couldn't understand this, so I asked him, "I received my PhD in 76, and since then, I have worked as a professor at FSU for two years, a consultant in Washington D.C. for three, and have two years of experience working at KEDI. I should at least be an associate professor." Then, he began persuading me by telling me, "A lot of people in their fifties are still assistant professors, Dr. Huh. You're young, so you can definitely start as one." I could not accept this. I told him I'd like to withdraw my acceptance of their offer and left the office.

This was an unexpected turn of events. I felt I shouldn't have given up on the opportunity since Dr. Hong took extra care to hand it to me. Even though I put forth a confident facade uttering my ultimatum at the dean's office, I was worried that I had blown the opportunity and diasppointed Dr. Hong. Fraught with worry, I sought my father-in-law's counsel. After hearing my situation, he told me, "You know, this isn't America. This is Korea. Maybe you should just accept the offer. Sometimes, you just lose a little." Although he told me to stick with my plan to go to Hanyang, my pride wouldn't allow me to go back to the dean's office and retract what I said. It was a dilemma.

A few days later, the dean called me back to his office. When I came in, he asked me how I knew Chairman Kim. I played dumb and told him, "Of course, I know of him, but I have no personal acquaintance with him." He seemed confused by my response and continued, "After you left, chairman called me and asked why I didn't hire you. He said you were a genius, and we should not let you escape. I've never seen the chairman so invested in hiring a professor."

Saying all of this, the dean made me an offer. "I will promote you to associate professor after the first semester." I could not refuse this time, so I accepted his offer and began working as an assistant professor. This was fall of 1982. At the time, the human resources policy for universities was that an associate professor must work for minimum of four years before being promoted to associate professor. Thankfully, through expediency, forms were sent stating that I began working as an associate professor in the spring of 83, but I did 'lose' six months of teaching experience because of it.

I had taken my first step in reaching my dream of becoming a professor. I was on my way to bringing new educational reform through introducing ISD and other computer systems into schools, industries and the military.

Founding Korea's First Educational Technology Department

Once I started teaching at Hanyang University, and it was now time to found the Educational Technology department. I met with Dr. Lee Su Won at the Department of Education to discuss exactly how to do this. At the end of our discussion, we agreed to recruit students for the new department among the incoming class in the Education department. To do so, the university selected twice the usual number of students and told them the school was recruiting students for a new department called Educational Technology. I also participated in informing the students about what Educational Technology was and what the possible employment prospects were after graduation for those who chose the field. At the end of our recruitment, we found out that out of sixty incoming students, exactly half of them chose to go into our new department. The Department of Educational Technology was thus founded with thirty new students.

Busy Spreading the Word about Educational Technology

Even though we had founded Educational Technology department, I was the only full-time professor in it. This meant I had to do almost everything, from coming up with the curriculum to recruiting professors for the department. I worked hard, and thankfully around this time, Dr. Kim Jong Yang returned to Korea after finishing his degree at Columbia. His return helped things move along faster, and our department slowly began to take shape. To the outsiders, however, the Educational Technology department must have seemed new and foreign. Many people were asking, "Exactly what does that department do?," and every time I was asked this question, I did my best to explain to them, but I found it difficult to make people fully understand the concept. This made me wonder how I could help people fully grasp the purpose of our department. Finally, I concluded I needed to address this issue through corporate training.

Opening the Computer Educational Research Institute and Corporate Training

When I was working on military training projects as a PhD student, the projects were sponsored by the Educational Technology Research Institute, which Dr. Morgan had founded. I decided I needed to create a similar research institute at Hanyang and to capitalize my experience in managing international projects and military projects. I envisioned using the educational technology approach to reform Korea's military, corporate and educational system with our research institute as the base. I felt I could use my previous experience working at Athena in Washington D.C. to do similar work for Korean corporations. Once my vision crystallized, it quickly established forward momentum in opening our research institute. We decided to name our institute the 'The Computer Educational Research Institute.' Later, it would be renamed the 'Institute for Educational Technology.'

Once our institute opened, I started working with Korean corporations on reforming corporate training. As I had done in the States, I lectured passionately about how Korean corporations will need to train their executives in the future. My lectures began with Hyundai Corporation, then I went on to work with Samsumg, LG, Ssangyong and other major companies.

Mistaken as a Female Employee at a Corporate Lecture

In 1980, it was very rare to see a female speaker giving a speech to a room full of male audience in a corporate setting. Once, I was invited to give a speech at a company training camp held at a suburban hotel. The speech was given to a group of HR executives from the company's subsidiaries. I was following a company employee into the lecture hall when he realized he had forgotten the laser pointer and had to go get it. I went into the lecture hall by myself and was walking toward the front row seats. Because it was a large hall full of people, I had to walk a bit of distance to get to the front of the room. As I was walking, a middle aged man from the audience stopped me and asked me to run an errand for him. I was so taken back but gained my composure and explained, "I'm sorry but I can't because I'm busy right now." I continued walking and the employee came back with my pointer. Soon, the presenter introduced me, and I began my lecture.

After the speech, I was leaving the hotel and was about to get into the company car waiting for me, when I noticed the same middle-aged man running towards me. He bowed his head several times and said, "I'm so sorry. I didn't know you were the speaker. I committed a huge imprudence. Please forgive me. I am really sorry." He looked very apologetic. There were also other people outside who were waiting to say hello to me. They seemed perplexed at what was happening and kept looking back and forth at the man and myself. Ignoring their curious looks, I smiled at him and told him it was ok. Relieved, he scratched his head and mumbled, "It's just that you're such a young woman" and walked away.

Developing the First Educational Software with Hyundai Electronics' CEO Jung Mong Hyun

As I gained more experience in corporate training, word spread and I received more invitations from corporations to work with them. I took these invitations as opportunities to promote the research fellows at our institute. I would tell them I was busy, but our student-researchers could come and speak instead. Gradually, this led to more project invitations coming directly to our institute. One of the first full-fledged projects we worked on was with Hyundai Electronics whose ceo at the time was Jung Mong Hyun, Hyundai Group's promising son.

This was in the mid 1980's when personal computer use was rising rapidly, and every PC manufacturing company began claiming theirs was the 'educational PC,' hoping it would increase their sales. I decided to gather up those who were in charge of PC's from different electronics companies and told them, "There is no point advertising your product as the educational PC because your computers don't have an educational software inside. It's false advertisement." I also paired this speech with a demonstration of our newly developed software. Soon, one company after another began showing their interest in our software, and Hyundai Eletronics was the first to work directly with us on this.

After we agreed to work together, I made an offer to Mr. Jung, "I will send you the best of my students to work on this project. In return, you should hire them as official Hyundai Electronics employees. You can send them back to our institute later when the project is done. They will develop an educational software for middle and high schools that Hyundai Electronics can use."

Mr. Jung gladly accepted my offer, which I made mainly because I was determined to find jobs for my research students. I am still thankful to him for agreeing to hire my students.

At this time, we were in the beginning stages of our work, and program development software was quite expensive. Some American software applications cost as much as $100K to develop a single program. Despite this high price, Mr. Jung gave us his full trust and didn't hesitate to purchase any software programs we told him we needed. When it came to key concept programs, it was customary to give a demo to the ceo. One time during one of our demo sessions, Mr. Jung came in with a cast on his foot which he had broken during a soccer game. Even with a cast, he was very

1   With Chairman Kim, his wife and governor of Kentucky.

2   At my Hanyang University office.

3   With Alexei, the head of Russia's INT.

4   At my home, with my students from the Institute.

happy and eager to evaluate our newly developed program. And with his full support, we were able to come up with multiple educational software programs. These were the very first ones to be developed by a Korean corporation.

Samsung SDS Aspires to Be EDS

At the time, the vice president at Korea's *Electronics* was Mr. Nam Gung Suk, who later became minister of Information and Communications. Most people know him as a 'Samsung man,' but there was a brief period of time when he worked at Hyundai. I met him when he was working at Hyundai, and thanks to this meeting, I was later able to secure a project with Samsung.

When Mr. Nam later became the ceo of Samsung SDS, he would tell his employees who were working on educational programs to "consult with Dr. Huh at Hanyang University" and some of his people from Samsung SDS came asking me to come up with a program. I told them, "We don't just make an educational program at a company's request. We have a systematic approach. We need to know what kind of curriculum Samsung needs and why, so we can analyze that information and come up with a goal and a vision. Then we will develop a program according to those goals." Whenever I asked such specific questions to the employees, they seemed burdened by them. However, I still needed this information to conduct my analyses and come up with the best program for them. After having a few conversations with SDS employees, I realized the company was trying to emulate EDS, an American company internationally famous for its comprehensive computer systems. So I told them, "I see that you guys are trying to become like EDS, which means you need to benchmark against them. I can help you do that." But they shook their head, and the leader of their group said, "That's impossible. EDS is already working with LG, and they started operating a local joint venture company called STM. We can't benchmark against EDS when they're already working with our competitor." I replied by asking them, "So who do you want to benchmark?" and they told me they were looking to benchmark against a second tier company that was a lot lower in ranking. I didn't understand their reasoning, so I asked how they could aspire to be like EDS, yet think it's ok to benchmark against a company that was far behind. I reiterated, "You should absolutely benchmark against EDS. It is not impossible, and I will make it happen."

Nothing Is Impossible.
Jerry Dawson Allows a Visit to His Company

I had an idea. Over the years, I became acquainted with many corporate figures by working as a corporate consultant. One acquaintance with whom I developed a friendship with was Dick Warmington. He was an American working as the ceo of Samsung HP Korea, a joint venture between Samsung and HP. I called him and asked him if he knew the ceo of STM. Luckily, Dick told me that he did. It seemed that most branch managers of foreign companies assigned in Korea knew each other very well. I got Mr. Dawson's phone number and gave him a cold call. I explained to him I was a professor in Korea consulting with Samsung SDS and asked if he could help Samsung benchmark against EDS. He gave me an unexpected response. He said to me, "Sumsung SDS and STM are competitors like a pitcher and a batter in baseball. Why should I help you do this?" I saw this wasn't going to be easy, and I began explaining to him in a calm voice, "Of course, I understand your position as the ceo of STM, and you're right that Samsung SDS and your company are competitors. But I would like you to forget for a moment that you are the ceo of STM, and listen to my request as the former executive member of EDS. As you know, EDS is a global consulting company dealing in systems integration. You can see how Samsung SDS could become a valuable client to EDS, which you consider your parent company. I think you can see why you should help me if you just looked at the big picture."

I utilized all the negotiation skills I had honed as a consultant back in Washington D.C., and thankfully, Mr. Dawson changed his answer to "yes." He even invited me to meet him personally. This confirmed to me the best way to work with an American business person is by employing American pragmatism.

I went see Mr. Dawson as we had agreed. The STM office was at the Twin Building in Yeouido, which also housed the LG Group's head office. When I entered his office, I saw a handsome blonde man in his early 40's looking out the window at Han River. When he saw me, he turned around and greeted me. As we sat down and drank tea, he pointed at a picture of an eagle hanging on a wall and asked me, "Do you know what this eagle symbolizes?" I hesitated a bit and said, "Isn't it a symbol for America?" Mr. Dawson answered, "Yes, it is a symbol of America, but also, an eagle never lives in a pack, and neither do I. I fly solo even though it is lonely." A powerful first move, I thought. As our conversation continued, I told Mr. Dawson about my work experience in America being a consultant to many companies, and he came to understand how badly I wanted to help Samsung SDS. He finally said to me, "After hearing what you have to say, it seems like I can't stop you from helping Samsung SDS benchmark against EDS, so I want to help you. From my experience working with them, Samsung always insists on doing things their way, the 'Samsung way.' I predict even if they benchmark against EDS, they will only use it as a reference point and ultimately go back to doing things their old way, which means not that much loss for STM even with my help. I will give you my full support, and I'll even lend you an STM ID so you can take a tour of our head office." With this shocking support, we were finally able to fly to the U.S. to visit the EDS head office.

Service Is More Important Than Technology

Before we took off for EDS's head office in the U.S., Mr. Dawson gave us some expert advice. He said, "Right now, the American company IBM is dominating the global computer industry. So, if a company like SDS gets a request from its client for a networking system, it will undoubtedly use IBM's system. This is not good because the client could be a government, a school or a company. What companies like SDS should do is analyze the client's request and then design the best program accordingly. It shouldn't simply install IBM's system and think they've finished the job. The reason why this happens is because SDS thinks of itself as a technology company. But a system integration company is not just a technology company. It's also a service company. Without the under-standing of this basic concept, SDS will not take away the key elements of the service industry even if they benchmark against EDS. For example, if they are consulting an oil company and think they might need to take a different approach than usual in coming up with a system, they should be willing to use an Apple system instead of IBM's. But they don't know how to do this. So, the point is, SDS needs to realize they are not a technology company, they are a service company."

I really agreed with his advice, and as we were touring EDS, I paid special attention to their key functions. The most impressive thing I saw was their data backup system. Their office space spanned multiple low-rise complexes, and we couldn't help but notice how impeccable their backup system was. It seemed as though it could withstand a nuclear attack.

Completing the 'Huh Unna Matrix'

After we got back from our EDS tour, I immediately began working on the "Capability matrix for systems integration task" so we could tangibly help Samsung SDS. The matrix I came up with then was later referred to as the '*Huh Unna* Matrix' by ceo Mr. Nam. On the X-axis, I listed all the necessary functions in executing our mission. On the Y-axis, I listed all the major capabilities needed for carrying out these functions. Putting both of them together got me the key capability points for a specific function, the intersecting point of the two axes. From this, I further divided the key capabilities into 'already obtained,' 'half obtained,' 'not yet obtained,' 'obtainable in a year' and 'obtainable with another capability' categories. I also specified each capability's level of urgency by giving a label 'very urgent,' 'eventually needed,' or 'need in a few years.' Lastly, I specified the optimal educational technique for each. Once this matrix was complete, we could get a very clear picture of what Samsung SDS needed to do now in terms of technology development and intensive courses for their system integration tasks. There were challenges along the way, but by visiting EDS, we learned a lot, and ultimately, we followed the ISD process and came up with the optimal educational program for Samsung SDS.

The Korean Army's Training and the Doctrine Command Project Cancelled at the Last Minute

This particular incident happened when Mr. Nam served as the vice president of Hyundai Electronics. At the time, our Computer Education Research Institute was working closely with Hyundai Electronics to develop various educational software programs, and in the process, our team became very close to Mr. Nam. One of the executive members under his management was from the military, and when he heard me talk about the results of my past projects working with the American military on computer-based education, he thought it would be great to apply the same to the Korean military. He connected me to the *Korean army*'s Training and Doctrine Command. I packed a bag full of CBT sample programs we had developed and drove down with my students to TRADOC in Gwangju, Jeollanamdo. We met with the three star general, commander Kim Jin Young, and there, I gave a demonstrative lecture to hundreds of officers. After my lecture, Commander Kim told me he thought the computer-based education would be useful for the army and ordered the staff to begin developing a program for them. Unfortunately, just as we were about to begin working on their program, Commander Kim was promoted to Army Chief of Staff and left TRADOC, and our project was cancelled. I was very disappointed, but one of the officers from an intelligence school near Seoul contacted me and told me he was interested in taking over the project. By this chance, we were able to salvage our project through this new agreement with an intelligence school.

The Rising Status of Our Department and Getting Our Students Employed

As a founder of the first Educational Technology department in Korea, I felt responsible for getting our graduates employed after they left the school. This led me to pursue any opportunity for a contract aggressively, be it with schools, corporations or the military, to raise the status and recognition of our department's work. For the first ten years after the initial founding of the department, I really poured my heart and soul into successfully completing all the projects *and* finding jobs for my students.

Maybe because of these efforts, our department's status slowly began to rise. Before our department was firmly established within the Korean academia, there were only two other university departments that were related to Educational Technology, the Department of Education and Educational Psychology. And it was the graduates from these two departments who had long dominated the Korean educational world. We had to put up with their snobbish attitude asking us, "Just what exactly is educational technology?" Some people were obviously condescending towards our department and called us 'a group of technicians.' I spent a lot of time trying to figure out a way to correct these misconceptions and realized that proving our worth by showing our success with projects would take too long. I needed something more immediate. Ultimately, I came up with the idea to turn our department into one that students would vie to get into. To do this, I needed a carrot to dangle in front of the students to lure them in. I figured the best carrot was offering hands-on experience and more importantly, promising employment prospects.

An Institute That Gives Monthly Stipend

I ran the Institute completely like a company. The payments we received for our projects were managed with full transparency, and we began paying monthly stipend to our students working at the institute. In the beginning, our projects were worth several thousand dollars, but as time went by, we started attracting projects that were larger in scale. Some of them were worth several hundred thousand dollars per a single project. This meant our students had the unique opportunity to go to school, get hands-on industry experience working on our corporate projects *and* earn a paycheck.

More importantly, as the manager of the Institute, I was quite successful at getting many of my students jobs at enviable corporations like Samsung and Hyundai. As a lot of our students made a smooth transition from school into the workforce, more students began showing interest in our department. About seven years after our department was established, one of the senior professors from the Department of Education, Dr. Lee Su Won came to see me at my office. He said to me, "I want to apologize for all the things that were said about your department that were incorrect. I hope you can forgive us. We didn't know what you guys really did. But I have to say, I have been watching your departmental work, and I've been very impressed and surprised. It made me realize Educational Technology is a very practical field much needed in our time. With that said, I have come to ask you for a favor. Many students in our department want to work at your Institute. It would be wonderful if you could accept some of these students."

Seeing people who used to ridicule our department as a 'field without any basis' now change their tunes and pay us such compliment meant the battle had truly shifted in our favor. It gave me great relief to know my hard work had finally paid off. Hanyang University's Education Technology department had made its mark. It became the first department from the College of Education to bring in large-scale projects and pay a monthly stipend to its students who participated in them.

Our Department's Duumvirate, President Kim Jong Ryang

The oldest son of Hanyang University's chairman, Kim Jong Ryang graduated from Columbia University in 1985 with a PhD in Educational Technology, and he returned to Korea. When he did, we joined our efforts and made a formidable duumvirate hiring new professors to be our successors. Dr. Kim was a very good singer, which wasn't surprising since his father, the chairman of Hanyang University, was also a very famous music composer. His sister Dr. Kim Myung Hee was also working at the Department of Education at Hanyang. With my unique tie to Chairman Kim made when I came to Hanyang, and working in proximity to both of his children, I developed a very special bond with this family.

Many Sparrows at the University

Chairman Kim preferred to hire professors who were fluent in English. Although I was not the only professor who spoke English fluently, whenever we had foreign guests visiting the school, he would ask me to show them around. The first time this happened, it was a distinguished guest from America, and I was paired with Dr. Kim Jong Ryang to escort our guest. At the time, I was a married woman with two children, and Dr. Kim was a single male, one year younger than me.

That night after we showed our guest around, I was at home when I got a call from Dr. Kim's sister and our co-colleague, Dr. Kim Myung Hee. As it was fairly late at night, I wondered what the call was about. Over the phone, Dr. Kim said to me in a giggly voice, "Dr. Huh, do you know what happened this afternoon? My brother and I were talking with our father, and my father asked my brother 'Why have you been hiding such a nice young lady all this time?' Apparently, he saw you escorting foreign guests with my brother at the dinner he hosted and mistook you for his girlfriend. I told him that you were a married woman with two kids, and he looked so disappointed. My brother was laughing so hard." It was such a funny incidence. Dr. Hong had surely mentioned I was married when he first introduced me, but Chairman Kim just didn't think the female professor whom he saw going with his son to greet their guests was the same professor that was introduced through Dr. Hong. I guess as a chairman, you can't remember every single professor working at the university. The silly incident, however, didn't end there, and it started a rumor among the chatty sparrows at school that the reason Dr. Kim Jong Ryang insisted on staying single well past the marrying age was because of me. But since it was just a rumor, there was nothing really I could do about it.

One Should Never Fix Their Hat String
under a Prunaria Tree

Having received his degree from prestigious Columbia University and being the son of the university chairman himself, I knew Dr. Kim Jong Ryang would not remain a regular professor. He would eventually become the chairman and probably the president of the university. In the meantime, after teaching as a professor in our department, Dr. Kim was chosen to be the head of the planning department. The position was an important one covering the entire administrative affairs at the school. One day, he came to see my office and told me he was planning an overnight gathering and a dinner party for all the professors. He wanted to see if I could give a lecture on the topic of educational reform and progressive teaching methods. My answer was an emphatic "No." At Hanyang, there were a lot of senior professors, especially in the Engineering and Medical schools. Even in other colleges, there were only a few professors who were younger than me. Knowing this, I didn't feel comfortable at all delivering the lecture because of how patriarchal Koran society still was. But despite my answer, Dr. Kim insisted, telling me how we must share the future paths Korean universities should take with all of our colleagues. He said in order to incite a fresh new wave of progress, a western educated person like me should deliver the lecture. I could tell his intentions were pure, and he was almost naive in his eagerness to help Hanyang move forward. Since I could no longer decline his emphatic request, I told him I would gladly speak at the event. And as predicted, the lecture caused a great outcry among the faculty. People were saying, "How dare a young woman like her try to lecture us?" and made slandering comments like, "Her institute is basically operating on the university subsidy!" and "Just because she has personal connection to the chairman, she thinks she can condescend us!" Soon after this lecture, Dr. Kim became the head of university. Even though Dr. Kim and I used to have frequent meetings to discuss our mutual concern and love for our department, I cut back on these meetings after I heard some of the angry comments that were made after my lecture. I think Dr. Kim also felt similar concerns because he didn't ask me to give another lecture after that. But being the subject of others' criticism and envy did teach me one lesson. I learned that, as an old Korean saying goes, "One should never fix their hat string under a Prunaria tree."

Over the years, Dr. Kim has earned the reputation as the most successful educator out of all whose parents were the founder of the university. Dr. Kim himself contributed greatly to Hanyang's becoming number five in the national ranking of universities, and he is known among other scholars for always being modest and respectful towards the elders.

Modesty Tops in Korea

"This isn't America." I learned this lesson over and over as I confronted the most baseless slanders and envy from my colleagues in the Korean academia. From this, I learned I must always act with great modesty in my profession. When I nominated Dr. Lee Young Duk as the first president of Korean Society for Educational Technology which I founded, the decision was in line with this modesty. I decided not to take on the president role until the third presidency.

After finally earning the respect of my peers, I founded the Korean Society for Industrial Education and nominated myself as the president. For its second president, I nominated Mr. Lee Jin See, who was the director of Hyundai's Human Resources Development. After him, I had different Human Development heads from major corporations like Samsung assume the presidency on a rotation basis. As the Industrial Education Society took root, universities across the country began creating Industrial Education departments. As Educational Technology grew steadily as a department, I surprisingly found out people were calling me 'the mother of Korea's Educational Technology.'

Ewha Womans University renamed its former Audio-Visual Education Department to Educational Technology, and soon, Andong University also founded its own Educational Technology department as well. Then Seoul National University and other major university followed suit, and most other university created their own version of the Educational Technology Department or major.

Cutting Edge IT Equipment
Even the Airport Customs Didn't Recognize

The Educational Technology department closely monitored new developments being made in the IT field. In the late 1980's, I traveled to many developed countries to purchase and bring back the newest IT equipment.

One gadget that was considered very revolutionary at the time was the floppy disk, which stored computer data. Today, nobody uses a 'floppy,' a flat square plastic dish you insert into the disc driver of your PC. Once, I went to America to buy an Apple floppy disk. The disc was selling at 450 dollars, an exorbitant price. When I came back to Korea, I had to take out the disc and show it to the customs officer at the airport. He took a good look at it, flipping it up and down and turning it. He seemed to think it was just a piece of metal and plastic, and without much enthusiasm, he let me pass with the disc. Unfortunately, the then cutting-edge gadget proved to lack durability and only lasted three months. Later, the laser disc I brought from England became so popular and wide-spread, they were literally distributed to and used by all the karaoke bars in Korea and became an overnight sensation. I was incredibly amazed at how fast the IT technology was evolving and becoming nearly ubiquitous.

As technology evolved, I kept working to raise the reputation of our department. I also continued working on implanting computer-based training at schools, companies and the military. Then in September 1987, I decided to take a sabbatical year and went to England to stay at the Cambridge University.

Enchanted by European Scent
in Cambridge

Being a Researcher at Darwin College

In 1987, I was nominated to participate in a program for research professors at England's Cambridge University. This was a joint program sponsored by the British Embassy in Korea and the British Council. I was very happy to be selected from a stiff competition, and considered myself very lucky. It was a precious opportunity to spend one full year working at a research institute on Cambridge's campus, with full finance and administrative cost covered by the British Council.

Cambridge University has a very different system from Korean universities. In Korea, we use the word 'university' to describe collegiate post-secondary institutions. We use 'college' to refer to separate schools underneath a university, like the (college of) Engineering School. In England, Oxford or Cambridge's colleges are independent universities, both are made up of several such colleges. For instance, Cambridge University has King's College, Queen's College and Trinity College, just to name a few. These colleges were founded in different years by different founders, and all their buildings are built in different styles. The colleges all

1 Me as an exchanged professor at Cambridge.
2 In front of Cambridge's Trinity College.
3 With David Rogers, director of British Council and the president of examiners of British Council exchange professors.

have separate majors within them, and they independently run their admissions. Students apply to the university, but the university only manages things on the administrative level. I was assigned to one of these colleges called the Darwin College, which was founded by Charles Darwin, father of the evolutionary theory. Darwin College didn't have an undergraduate program and only offered graduate courses. My days as a researcher would be spent at the oldest building where Darwin himself lived.

Dinner Time Full of Live Tradition

As I began my life at Darwin, I quickly realized that dinner time was very important. To explain, eligibility for sitting at dinner was reserved only for international scholars like myself, faculty at the college and their invited guests. At seven thirty in the evening, people would come to the second floor of the cafeteria, which had long dining tables, each of which could seat tens of people. I'd heard from someone I had heard from someone before coming to Cambridge that to get a master's degree here, you need to have eaten at the cafeteria a certain number of times, and I remembered not understanding what that meant.

Eating dinner at this dining hall was a great opportunity to meet all kinds of international scholars. I got to hear many interesting stories from scholars from many fields and specialties. There was the astronomer studying meteors, a meteorologist specializing in ice caps in the North Pole, and an architect whose forte was the 17th century cathedrals. It was a truly special learning experience you could only get at a Cambridge dining table. Another aspect of the dining experience was the weekly formal dinner where everyone had to wear their college gowns. Normally, people only wear their college gown once at their graduation, but at Cambridge, they wore it every week. I had to call Dr. Kim and ask him to send the gown to participate in the dinners. After dinner, we didn't part right away either. Instead, we would retire downstairs to a lounge type

TWELFTH
NIGHT

OR WHAT YOU WILL

by
William Shakespeare

1

2

1   One of Shakespeare's play from Cambridge University.
2   Shakespeare's hometown 'Stratford upon Avon.'

room, sit in groups of three's and five's, drink our tea and continue with our discussions from dinner. Dinner time at Cambridge was a time to experience a luxurious tradition and intellectual discussions unique to Cambridge.

Watching a Shakespeare Play in His Hometown

At Darwin, I was living next to Nadia who was from Saudi Arabia and Indira who was from Bangladesh. We ladies would often socialize and see films together. One time, I tried horseback riding at Nadia's suggestion, but it wasn't my kind of activity. Eventually, I chose to return to my long time hobby, which was aerobic dancing.

I'd always thought if I ever visited England, I would see a Shakespearean play done in its original English, costumes and stage setting. Being here offered me the perfect chance to do that. The very first play I saw was *Twelfth Night*. The play was presented on an outdoor grass field outside one of the Colleges. I saw most of the plays alone because it was difficult to find someone who was free during the play times, and it was convenient to go watch a play whenever I wanted. The second play I saw was *Julius Caesar*, which like other plays, was performed by Cambridge students and was not a real professional performance. Most people in the audience were young students who were not shy about clapping or shouting cheers in the middle of the play. As I really wanted to watch a high-quality play while I was in Shakespeare's hometown, I went to Stratford one day. With other tourists, I went on a little tour of Shakespeare's birthplace and went along the Avon River. The play I watched was at a playhouse on the riverside. I watched *Twelfth Night* again, and later I returned to watch *Romeo and Juliet*. Having twice visited Shakespeare's birthplace and strolled the streets filled with Elizabethan architecture, I was glad to have checked off one of the boxes on my literature-major bucket list.

Cambridge, a Place of Formality

One thing that struck me as an unnecessary formality during my days at Cambridge was their invitations. In America, when there was a luncheon or dinner among faculty members, the invitation was given through a simple phone call. In England, an invitation from one faculty member to another from the same or different College was always given through a formal letter. The invitation letter was so formal it resembled a Korean wedding invitation with its silver lining along the edges. The letter had the names of invitees, and more formal ones even came with an assigned seating chart. Because of how formal they were, receiving one always felt pleasant and very special.

An OECD Seminar That Made Me Feel the Pains of Coming from a Weaker Country

The British Council that invited me to England arranged for me to attend an international seminar related to my field. It was going to be held in Glasgow and sponsored by OECD (Organization for Economic Cooperation and Development) on the topic of educational computers. The seminar was for OECD members only, which meant technically, as a Korean, I wasn't eligible to attend, and I had to go as an invitee of the British Council. The seminar turned out to be a small one with less than fifty attendants, and another Japanese attendee and I were the only Asians there. But unlike me, the Japanese attendee was a legitimate member of OECD. After the seminar, I was in the lobby having a drink when the Japanese attendee came up to me. Knowing that I was from Korea, he asked me with a smile how I came to the event. Even though he had a smile on, I could tell he was insinuating I didn't really have a right to be there. This annoyed me a little, but since I didn't have a very good reply, there was nothing much for me to say in reply to his rude question. Then later, an incident happened which really upset me. During one of the discussions, I raised my hand to ask a question. When I did, the host of the seminar who was Australian said to me, "Actually, you are here as an observer and a non OECD member. Would you mind just observing our seminar?" I was so angry. Of course she was just doing her job, but at the time I didn't understand. I had never been treated this way at any international meeting. I wondered how someone like her could be working at an international organization like OECD. I would have liked to say something in return but technically, she was right, and I just sat in silence. I realized then how influential our national power is in shaping to perceptions. (This was such a generation-specific incident considering Korea is now a member of OECD and world's 15th biggest economy).

Cool Friends Edna and Martin

After getting a little upset over what had happened with the Australian host, I went back the meeting for the subcommittee discussion. The subcommittee I was assigned to had six members. There were two Danish and two English members, one Finnish member and myself. The two from Denmark were Edna and Martin, and Harold was from Finland. They were all school commissioners, whereas the two English members were professors. We started discussing different ways of using the computer, the problems that came with it and possible solutions to these problems. During the discussion, our group members kindly told me I could speak up freely. This made me feel better than before, and we ended up having a very interesting discussion. Back at the hotel, the six of us were sitting at the same table, and someone brought up the rude comments made by the host. Everyone said they were mortified by what was said and told me to forget the whole 'ignorant' behavior. The Danish lady member Edna was even more upset than I was, and handsome Martin agreed with her sentiments. After spending two days with these guys, working on the same team and touring and participating in discussions together, we all became close friends. At the end of the event, Edna and Martin told me to come visit them in their home country Denmark.

A Danish Gentleman with Three Adoptive Korean Children

Not too long after the seminar, Edna and Martin invited me on a four day trip to Denmark. They told me they would take turns to show me around. Denmark is shaped like several peninsulas connected together, and it takes time to get around. My friends took me to Aarhus University and other places relevant to educational technology they thought I would be interested in. We also visited IBM Denmark, the training headquarters for the toy company Lego and the Danish Bank. It was December, and when I got there, Martin greeted me in a very thick leather jacket. He came to pick me up in his car, and I was going to stay at his house for a few days. Instead of going straight to his home, he told me there was someone he really wanted me to meet and brought me to his office. As I saw the short little trees outside his office building and cold frosted floors inside, I suddenly became aware I was in cold Scandinavia.

Inside the building, two very kind looking colleagues of Martin greeted us and offered me a warm handshake. They brought tea for us to drink, and one of them grabbed a photo from Martin's desk and showed it me. In the photo, were three smiling Asian girls. Martin's colleague said to me, "I adopted all these girls from Korea." I was so surprised, I asked, "Three, really?" He then explained the whole story to me, and it was really touching. He told me he had adopted the first girl, but being all alone, his daughter was always lonely. So he decided to adopt a second daughter. But even after that, the girls still felt alienated among their white classmates at school so he decided to adopt a third one. "Being three, they sort of formed a power-group, and now they get along great with other friends at school and even overpower them. Haha." I couldn't help but feel deep respect for the compassion and love he had. When we arrived at Martin's home, it was late night, and we were greeted by his wife, his twin sons and his daughter. His house was decorated with beautiful Christmas ornaments. Martin's wife was a school teacher and a very mild-mannered lady who valued keeping a happy harmonious family. We ate dinner and spent a couple of hours in their living room eating home-made pies, talking about Danish Christmas customs and listening to stories about their children.

Denmark's Astoundingly Advanced IT Technology

On the second day, we decided to visit Aarhus University and take a look at their Engineering School's video conferencing equipment. For those who aren't familiar, video conferencing technology allows people to have a face-to-face conversation over long distances using computer monitors. At the time, Aarhus University's Engineering School was working with IBM Denmark on developing this technology (This technology is by now old news and very common, but back then, it was in its early stages of development). I was led by the professor in charge and told to sit at a desk. In front of the desks, there were two cameras. One was pointed at me while the other one was pointed at a pile of files in front of me. Suddenly, the TV screen in front of me came on, and an IBM technician from another city appeared. We said "hello" to each other, and as I wrote something on a piece of paper that was in front of me, he seemed to be reading what I was writing. On my screen, I could also see what he was writing on his paper. This was an amazing technology that would enable classes to take place with an instructor who was a long distance away. The next thing we saw was the video compressor. This was a machine about the size of a refrigerator and had computer chips inside. Its function was to compress and digitalize analogue video data and transfer it. I was so impressed by the technological accomplishments this small country had achieved. A lot of people know Denmark as an agriculturally focused country, but they are also advanced in creative designs and cutting edge technology, and their farmers use a lot of these technological tools in farming. A very well-known luxury audio equipment brand Bang and Olufsen is also Danish, and the famous Opera House in Sydney, Australia was also designed by a Danish architect.

Lego Blocks as a Creative Learning Tool

After visiting the university, we headed to the Lego company in the afternoon. The employees at Lego looked at these toy blocks as more than just toys. They looked at them as creative educational tools (Nowadays, many Korean schools fostering progressive teaching methods use Lego blocks, but back then, no one did). When we got there, we saw that there were people from the Danish Ministry of Education there who had come to learn about the principle behind electric cars using these blocks, computer chips and other electric equipment. This was such an impressive sight to me. The staff members were demonstrating teaching tools and materials that were developed for specific teaching levels. It was great to observe this live on-site training at a place I'd only previously considered a toy company. Later when I visited a few different Danish primary schools and also English schools, I saw a lot of Lego blocks were placed in classrooms to be used as teaching tools. These schools were teaching the children to nurture their creativity. The children were allowed to explore and expand their individual sense of curiosity by playing with the blocks, and they could come to understand everyday technologies in their lives by experimenting with them. The next day, we went to the birthplace of the famous Danish author *Andersen*, saw his house and went to the beach that had a statue of the heartbroken mermaid from one of his works *The Little Mermaid*.

Afterwards, it was time to go to Copenhagen. We got on a big ship in our car, parked the car and walked to the passenger's quarters. On my tour of Denmark, I noticed that Danish facilities and transportation were very convenient to use, and very clean and safe. These seemed to be basic principles on which the Danish society was built. On our visit to the primary school, I noticed the classroom doors looked very sturdy and asked the school principal about them. He explained to me that Danish primary schools had classroom doors that were triple-coated to prevent fire from spreading to other rooms. "This way, if there is ever a fire, it is immediately contained." I was once again reminded of their scientific inclination and cultural adherence to its principles.

Wife in the Living Room and Husband in the Kitchen

In Copenhagen, Edna was waiting for me. Since Edna was going to take over and show me around from this point on, we headed to her home first to meet her husband. Her husband was an architect, and she told me he had designed their house too. When we got there, her husband Laas was in the kitchen wearing an apron and preparing our dinner.

Edna took me around and gave me a tour of the house. Their house had a nice library, a large work studio for Laas, and an inviting and comfortable living room. The design had the combined elements of Danish pragmatism and ultra-modern minimalism. Shortly after, their daughter who was going to university came home and joined us at the dinner table, and we began eating. Our chef of the day kindly placed our steak and shrimp on our plates, and all three of us complimented him on how delicious the food was. Laas seem pleased and poured himself a glass of wine. Laas was a very kind man who suited his stylish and warm-hearted wife very well.

The next morning, Edna and I went to visit a technical high school which was very well equipped with computers and then went to a bank that had a great online infrastructure. After, we went to the Museum of Contemporary Art. At the museum, there was an exhibition of Edna's favorite Danish abstract artist. Even though I wasn't familiar with the artist, I really enjoyed his sculptures and colors and designs of his works. After the museum, Edna took me to an unexpected place. It was an old castle that was a setting in Shakespeare's *Hamlet*. It was shaped like a circular spiral moving upward, and inside of the castle was dark and bluish in color, reminiscent of the tragic character and fate of prince *Hamlet*.

The next morning, we did a tour of some educational institutions, and in the afternoon, we got to look around downtown Copenhagen. As we were strolling around Edna said to me, "Too bad the famous Tivoli Park is closed for the winter. It's a must-see."

In the evening, Martin joined Edna, her husband and me, and we went to see an opera. Everyone got dressed, finally and we headed to the Royal Opera House in downtown to see *La Boheme*. As we sat down in our seats and were waiting for the show to begin, we heard loud noises coming from the entrance. It turned out that on that same evening, the mother of Queen of Denmark had come to watch the show. What's more shocking, she was seated in the same row as our group, so we ended up watching the opera with real royalty.

Looking Around English Universities

After my worthwhile tour of Denmark, I returned to England to find out the British Council had arranged for me to take a tour of British universities. The itinerary said I was going to visit University of NewCastle, University of Edinburgh and University of Aberdeen, all the universities with a lot of research activities in the Educational Technology department. I got on the train and headed for NewCastle University, which was in the farthest northern part of England. After, I travelled to Scotland to make my way to University of Edinburgh and on to Aberdeen. After my tour, I had a chance to stop and take a look around York, Durham and Ely.

Once Thriving Industrial City NewCastle

NewCastle is an industrial city that was at the height of prosperity during the English Industrialization. However, by the end of the twentieth century as the world entered the Information Age, long shadows of decline loomed over the city. University of NewCastle was located in the city center, and like other universities in a similar location, its campus was scattered throughout different buildings and did not have the romantic atmosphere Cambridge did.

I went to meet with the head professor of their Educational Technology department. As I listened to him explain the school's programs and looked around the facilities, I realized they were much farther ahead in their research than Hanyang. They had already reached the later stage in developing their educational videodiscs. Since the university was trying to develop different programs to attract international students, they gave me a promotional pamphlet and asked me to promote their masters programs to our Hanyang graduates. Though the school seemed to have great facilities and programs for our students to come and study, they didn't offer a lot of scholarship.

English Doesn't Work in Edinburgh:
Scottish and Pinchas Zukerman

My first impression of Edinburgh getting off the train was very different from the one I had at NewCastle. I was walking around the downtown area before checking into my hotel when I saw a McDonalds and went in to have my lunch. The restaurant was full of tourists. After ordering my meal, I sat down and started reading some of the tourist leaflets lying on the table. One leaflet jumped out at me. It listed different performances going on around the area and said there was a charity show at seven thirty that evening by *Pinchas Zukerman* at a theater that was sponsored by *Princess Diana*. It also said the regular seats were sold out, but you could call and reserve a balcony seat. I didn't mind a balcony seat at all to watch *Zukerman*'s performance. I was so excited.

After finishing my burger, I hurried to find a pay phone and called to reserve my seat at the theater. I hailed a cab to my lodging and was surprised to find the cab driver had dropped me off at a stunningly beautiful 2-storey residence. I double checked the sign at the front and saw I was at the right place. It was a very neat house, which was very different from the place I stayed at in NewCastle.

I changed and went back out to check out a nearby city square, trying to absorb the city's atmosphere. As I walked around, I noticed I wasn't understanding what people were saying around me. I felt like *Alice* in Wonderland not being able to understand anything when I knew they all were speaking in English. Later, I learned that I was in Scotland, which was part of Britain but where people were culturally distinct from the English. I also learned they had a strong sense of ethnic pride, and most people spoke Scottish rather than English, which explained my inability to understand anything.

The performance by *Zukerman* was fantastic. He played and conducted at the same time, and the audience went wild. It was lovely to have such an unexpected opportunity to catch Zukerman in Edinburgh.

Young Koreans at University of Edinburgh

The next morning, I headed to University of Edinburgh. One of the professors I had met at the OECD seminar was there, and he came to meet me. He then gave me a very thorough explanation and all the information I wanted from the university.

It was evening time when I got off the train at Aberdeen. After I checked in at the hotel, I decided to go for a quick walk around the hotel. The streets, the stone houses and the cathedrals all seemed extremely clean and organized that it almost felt lifeless like there was no one living there.

The next morning when I went back to the university, two young Korean guys were waiting for me. They were from the *Korea Military Academy* and were working on their PhDs. One of them was majoring in Educational Technology and told me he had already known about me from reading my book. I was very glad to meet people from my own country in Edinburgh.

The school's Educational Technology department was deeply committed to its research to develop software programs. Led by a young Korean professor, they were trying to make programs that were individualized to cater to different student levels and learning styles. It was a little like trying to come up with methodologies for the Socratic teaching for the entire student body: a modeling process that would take a long time and a lot of work to complete.

Woman of Steel, Prime Minister Thatcher

When I was at Cambridge, the English Prime Minister Margaret Thatcher was strongly pushing for educational reforms. The English economy had hit an all time low due to repeated strikes, and Thatcher ultimately played a vital role in revitalizing the country's economy through her uncompromising stance. She was also equally passionate about reforming the educational system. Once when she visited her alma mater, Oxford

University, a group of disgruntled students threw eggs at her face. Many people disagreed with her views on educational reform as she was trying to move England away from the traditional approach where students were not graded on a curve and didn't have excessive pressure to perform academically. Instead, Thatcher wanted to introduce a more strict evaluation system believing it would ultimately help boost the country's economic competitiveness. She also wanted universities to become independent and come up with their own funding. In turn, teachers came together in opposition, and in particular, universities like Oxford and Cambridge that produced the country's top academics and intellectuals did not stomach this well at all. In their eyes, these universities were purely academic entities that should never accept corporate money for their research. Thatcher was very disliked within the academia, but she did not bat an eyelash and stood by her agenda. After all, she had said that since everyone has different self-interest, politicians must remain unswayed by any group. I was impressed by the way she stood her ground to achieve her vision. Some people who watched me build the institute at Hanyang and push forward with multiple projects called me Huhcher, and I certainly didn't mind this nickname.

Flaming the Fire of
Korean Cyber Education

Meeting the Head of German Educational Institute
Deter Kaam at a Sydney Conference

After my one year sabbatical in England, I came back to Hanyang. In the spring of 1990, the WCCE (World Conference on Computer Education) was held at *Darling Harbor* in Sydney, Australia. I was invited to attend this event by the president of WCCE, Dr. Sandra Wells of Melbourne University.

The convention center was located right on Sydney harbor. Over two thousand attendees at the conference were busily making their way to their sessions. At the conference, I had a chance to reconnect with some of my foreign friends I had met previously at various other international conferences.

Being in Sydney, I couldn't miss the opportunity to attend an opera at the famous Opera House. On the last day of the conference, I was able to get my hands on a ticket to Gaetano Donizetti's *Lucrezia Borgia*. I found my seat and sat down to realize the seat next to mine was empty. I wondered, "How can there be an empty seat to a sold-out show?" As I was

1 Me giving a topic presentation at the Online Educa Korea Conference.
2 With Deter Kaam, director of Online Educa Berlin.
3 Me and a foreign professor in discussion at Online Educa.
4 With the hostess of an international conference held in Thailand.

waiting for the opera to begin, a middle-aged man came rushing in and sat down next to me. We looked at each other and said hello. From his accent, I could tell he was neither American, English, nor Australian. When the bells rang signaling the starting of the show, he pointed at my chest and asked, "Are you attending the WCCE too?" I realized then I was still wearing the name plate from that day's conference. A little embarrassed, I told him I was and removed my tag. The man reached into his pocket and handed me his business card. Right then, the second bell rang and the lights went off. I took a look at the card, which said his name was Deter Kaam. He was a director at a German educational institute.

During the intermission, Mr. Kaam asked me to get a drink at the café with him. I stepped outside, and he brought us each a glass of champagne and handed me my glass. We introduced ourselves, and the conversation turned to the topic of Germany's unification.

Deter told me that he was the director at an institute in Munich called FWU. FWU was a government organization that produced and distributed educational materials for all of Germany's educational institutions, from primary, secondary, post-secondary to vocational.

He told me that most of the educational materials they made were videos, films and computer software programs. He explained that his institute was quite large. After the reunification, he told me, it expanded to service all the institutions in the eastern part, and also provided materials to institutions overseas. Since my own institute did similar work, our conversation continued.

A Reunion on the Way to Czechoslovakia

I was on my way to *Prague* to attend the East-West Educational Technology seminar in Czechoslovakia (This was before Czech Republic and Slovakia separated). I was about to transfer onto a flight to Prague at the Frankfurt Airport when I ran into *Deter* unexpectedly. He told me he

1 Giving a keynote speech at a conference in Pretoria, South Africa.
2 Attending a dinner at the conference in Pretoria.
3 With the president of University of Pretoria.
4 Children of South Africa in Johannesburg.

was going to the same seminar. On the flight, we started chatting which made time go by quickly. The seminar was a big success with all the attendees leaving satisfied, and they decided FWU would sponsor the next seminar which would be held in Munich.

'Online Educa Korea' Accelerates the Founding of Cyber University

Online Educa Berlin or OEB was an international conference held annually on distance learning. It first started in Berlin, Germany in 1995.

This conference was co-sponsored by a German company ICWE and FWV with the support of Germany's Ministry of Education and other educational authorities of the European Union. There were nearly two thousand educational experts from one hundred countries attending the first conference, and I was there to represent Korea. OEB's size and their work were clearly impressive. When I returned to Korea, I thought to myself, "Could we hold an event like that in Seoul?" Determined to make this happen, I began working on launching the Korean version of OEB. It took a lot of footwork visiting many corporations and asking for their sponsorship. In 1996, my work paid off, and we held the 'Online Educa Korea.'

Online Educa Korea was sponsored by several major Korean corporations and supported by *Joong Ang Daily newspaper*. Under the banner of 'Information Technology and Educational Revolution Open Education Online,' we held the conference for two days at the Posco building in Gangnam's Daechi area. Experts in the field of online education from thirteen countries including the United States, Finland, Australia, Germany, England, Belgium and Japan attended the event, which acted as a catalyst in later creation of Cyber University in Korea. Furthermore, with KT's support, it successfully connected thirteen global educational sites through video-conference. All in all, the conference was praised for presenting a new model for an international academic event for the information era.

Preaching the Importance of Online Education

After the conference, I spent a lot of time preaching the importance of online education to those within the academia. I was invited to speak at many international conferences including in South Africa and Asia about online education. Later, when I entered the National Assembly, I also promoted online communication and video-conferencing, and as a result, more people began to understand its significance.

Receiving the Presidential Nomination for the Advisory Committee and Servicing My Country

Taking Part in the Informatization Promotion Committee under President Kim Young Sam's Administration

President Kim Young Sam left a huge legacy in the history of Korea's IT, and during his term, he helped Korea become a new global IT power. All of this began when the government took the then Ministry of Communications and expanded it into the Ministry of Information and Communication. President Kim aspired to become an 'Information-oriented president,' and throughout his term, he reiterated informatization was 'the key to increasing Korea's national competitiveness.'

The Ministry of Information and Communication enacted laws intended to accelerate Korea's informatization and provide it with legal and systematic support. In April 1996, an Informatization Promotion Committee was created to deliberate on promotional policies for informatization and Korea's IT industry. The prime minister was appointed to chair the committee that would include 25 members, including ministers from each department, the secretary general of the National Assembly and the minster of the National Court Administration. There would be six civilian members, and I was included in that group with a few ceos of venture companies. Later, when I became a whom an assembly woman I consulted with the young entrepreneurs with when I worked during this time about other IT-related matters.

A New World: Cyber-Space and EduNet

At this time, *Al Gore* was America's vice president and Chief of Information Officer (CIO), and he'd said, "In the future, the most powerful country will be the one that builds the first information highway for its citizens to enter the cyber space and create value."

I also advocated building schools in cyberspace and came up with the concept of 'Education within cyberspace' for the first time in Korea. To make this happen, our institute focused on developing cyber educational programs.

In trying to create Gore's information highway in Korea, the Informatization Promotion Committee came up with *the* key national computer traffic network that could connect 144 major cities in the country. The network was composed of five computer networks, including the administrative network, national security network, banking network, educational network called EduNet and the public security network. Out of these, I led our institute in creating the EduNet.

President Kim's Tears That Touched My Heart

While I was working on the committee, I was also busy giving lectures at companies about the importance building an information highway and trying to spread the notion. I was also invited to give similar lectures for presidents and vice-presidents of schools sponsored by the Korea Office of Education and for the public sector too. Even though I was busy, I accepted as many requests as I possible, both in and out of Seoul.

On the last day of his office, President Kim invited me and nine other members of the advisory committee to the Blue House for a luncheon. Usually, these kinds of meetings hosted by the president had over a hundred guests who all ate at several round tables. But that day, it was a very small luncheon of 'Kal-gooksoo,' president's favorite chopped noodles, and everyone was sitting face to face with the him at a single table. After our meal, we were all drinking tea when the president said with tears in his eyes, "You know, during my term, I had many supporters by my side, and now it's only my wife who's by my side." This was the first time I saw the vulnerable and truly human side of President Kim.

Touring the Country as a Member of the President's Educational Reform Committee

When the next President Kim Dae Jung took office, I was appointed as a member on his Educational Reform Committee. The president of Sambo Computers was picked as the chairman of the committee's IT leg, and I was the chair for its Educational Reform leg. Then later in the administration, our committee merged with the Educational Reform Evaluation Committee.

Over three years and two administrations, I took three rounds of visits to sixteen Education Offices across Korea to conduct evaluations. The focus of my evaluation was the area of education information. I met with superintendents and conducted a demonstrative evaluation of affiliated offices and schools within the jurisdiction.

As I conducted the evaluations from 1997 to 1999, I gradually adjusted my annual goals. In the first year, I focused on making sure all the schools in the country were equipped with PCs. The next year, the goal was to train the teachers to use PCs so they were prepared to train their students. To

Receiving the letter of appointment for the committee from
President Kim Young Sam.

do this, we included computer skills as a component of teacher evaluation criteria and gave teachers a personal incentive to learn the skills. In the third year, we focused on making sure that each school had an internet-based computer network.

Sending PCs to Schools by Using Unused Coin Money from Public Telephones

Getting PCs to every school in Korea required a huge budget, and there was not enough money in government's budget to accomplish the objective. As we were thinking about ways to come up with enough money, the Communications Department had an idea. They suggested using the free revenue collected from public telephones to pay for the computers (Free revenue is the portion of the money a person puts into the pay phone but doesn't get to use) We agreed this was a great idea and managed to persuade Korea Telecom to let us to use this money. I also convinced companies like Samsung, Hyundai and Sambo to make computer donations to schools and send their technicians to train the teachers and students in the school's new computer room. Soon, we generated a kind of computer boom, and schools across the country came up with their own computer room, and teachers and students started learning computer skills.

Even though all schools had their own PCs, I found many schools weren't actually using their computers, and a lot of the computer rooms were locked up. When I asked the school principal about this, they often told me there weren't enough qualified teachers or they didn't want the students to damage the computers. More than anything, we needed well-trained teachers, and we began developing training programs and encouraging teachers to get certified.

Working on the Presidential Advisory Committee for Science and Technology

Even though the Educational Reform Committee reported directly to the president, my work wasn't face-to-face with the president. Only when I got appointed as a consultant on the Committee for Science and Technology, it was a much smaller body of only 10 members, and I got to work more closely with the president.

President Kim Dae Jung was a great proponent of women's rights and ordered each advisory committee to have at least ten percent women members in it. Prior to this, there were only a very few women on these committees. One of the female members who joined the council was Dr. Kim Myung Ja from Sookmyung Women's University. However, soon after in 1999, she was appointed to the Ministry of Environment which left her seat vacant on the committee. I came to fill in that position.

The President and I Are Alumni of Cambridge

I'd actually met President Kim long before he became president. In 1992, he ran for presidency against Kim Young Sam and lost. He then left politics and went to study in England. He returned to Korea in 1994 and founded the Asia-Pacific Peace Foundation and worked as its chairman. The following year, he came back to politics by forming the National Conference and presiding as its president. In November 1997, he joined forces with a politician from the Chungchung Providence named Kim Jong Pil, created the DJP coalition and began promoting himself as the 'prepared president' on TV forums. All of this led Kim to win the next presidential election.

In England, he stayed at Cambridge University as a guest scholar. We met once during one of the Cambridge reunions in Seoul when I happened to have been seated next to his table. This was the first time I'd seen him in person, and like most people at the time, I thought of him as a veteran politician who was a fighter and a champion for what he believed in. When I started talking to him, however, I noticed that he was very gentlemanly with a great sense of humor and very mild-mannered. And I was greatly impressed by his public speaking. That day, he gave a speech, and watching him speak at the podium, I was surprised at his flawless speech. He seemed to be a genius in public speaking.

Meeting Mrs. Lee Hee Ho
Through the Information Movement

I had met the first lady Mrs. Lee Hee Ho through our mutual involvement in the Information Movement. While I was still a professor, I founded a corporation called 'Women, Information & Culture 21' to help improve women's informatization skills. As informatization progressed, women were lagging behind men in catching on, and I couldn't just sit and let this happen. Then a magazine called *Imagine* (I borrowed the title of the magazine from a famous *Beatles'* song) was published with a similar goal, and it was the first web magazine aimed at female readers.

For one of the seminars held for women on this topic of informatization, we invited Mrs. Lee Hee Ho as a keynote speaker. With her lifetime of work on women's rights, she was the perfect candidate for delivering the speech. Even though she didn't know me, she graciously accepted our invitation, and this is how we first met. We discussed my idea about giving computer training to kids at juvenile centers to help them become computer teachers after their release, and she really liked it. Graciously, Mrs. Lee gave me a lot of help and even got the Ministry of Justice to lend me support.

1   With the first lady Mrs. Lee Hee Ho at the Blue House.
2   First lady speaks at "Women, Information & Culture 21" foundation, where
    I was the president.

Entering Politics as a Proportional Representative for Information and Communication Technology

The Advisory Council for Science and Technology committee has a meeting with the president once every three months. At the meeting, one of the members presents and afterwards, the president gives his opinion or asks questions. Sometimes, if it's necessary, he gives specific orders to ministers. Once, it was my turn to speak, and my speech had a lot of jargon about information communication education. When the president gave his response, I was surprised and amazed to find that his response far surpassed my level of expertise on the subject. I already knew he was an avid reader, but he had a detailed understanding which was incredibly impressive. After our meeting, I heard some people say, "Judging by the president's response today, it seems like he considers you important." I didn't think much of their comment and just smiled.

Then, not too long before the National Assembly election was about to take place, assembly member Mr. Han Hwa Gab asked me to meet him. I met him at a Chinese restaurant at the 63 Building in Yeoido. We sat down, and he asked me, "What do you think about going into politics?" I was so surprised and told him, "A novice like me, I don't think I can last in politics. I think I will stick with teaching." This is how we ended our conversation that day, but a while later, I received a phone call from the chairman of the election polling committee asking me if I would consider being a proportional representative on the National Assembly. With all the invitations to join the world of politics, I decided to talk to my University President Mr. Kim Jong Ryang about it. After serious consideration, he told me he too thought I should stay at school. I made up my mind and let the Democratic Party know that I wasn't interested.

Soon afterwards, Mrs. Han Myung Sook, a long time friend of President Kim Dae Joong and who'd returned from America just before the election asked me the same thing. She asked, "You've worked for the government as a consultant. How did you like that?" I answered, "As an advisor, sometimes I felt very limited in what I could do. Even when I had a great idea, it was ultimately up to the public officials to decide what they wanted to do with it." She listened, "What do you think about you turning your visions to reality by joining a government party and becoming a member of the National Assembly?" With this convincing argument, I was sold. Eventually, Dr. Kim also agreed I should accept this offer.

Finally, after three solicitations, I accepted the offer and entered the 16th National Assembly as the 11th proportional representative for the Millennium Democratic Party.

After I became a National Assembly member, a fellow representative Mrs. Shin Nak Gyun told me, "The president asked me to recruit you, but I told him you're quite proud of your job and won't come into politics." Mr. Han Hwa Gap also jokingly asked me, "How come you didn't say yes when I asked you?" When the president nominated me as the eleventh member, Mrs. Han Myung Sook called me right away, "Dr. Huh, this is a miracle because you're the eleventh. Can you do me a favor and not act too chummy with me at the assembly?" When I asked her why, she said, "There are other women representatives that I've been close with who didn't make it, and I don't want them to feel betrayed by our friendship."

Receiving the President Kim Dae Jung's nomination for the Advisory Committee for Science and Technology.

Visiting a juvenile center with the President Kim Dae Jung and the first lady.

Act 5

Receiving My Call to Work
as a Member of
the National Assembly

Two roads diverged in a yellow wood.

And sorry I could not travel both and be one traveler,

long I stood and looked down as far as

I could to where it bent in the undergrowth.

Then took the other, just as fair.

...

I shall be telling this with a sigh

somewhere ages and ages hence.

"Two roads diverged in a wood, and I took the one less traveled by,

and that has made all the difference."

— Robert Frost, *The Road Not Taken*

Founding the IPAIT

Three Objectives as Novice Congresswoman

Proportional representatives in the National Assembly were a select a number of experts chosen from certain fields and affiliated with a political party. These representatives provided input in drafting bills that required a higher level of expertise. They would also speak on behalf of the party on these topics. I was appointed as my party's expert on science, technology and information.

I decided it was important for me to present myself as a fresh-faced politician from a university background untainted by conventional politics. So I came up with three personal principles to live by as I began my new job as a representative of the assembly.

First, I wanted to be a representative who continued to learn and educate herself. Two, I would always maintain my image as a transparent politician. Three, I would help raise our national status and power through information communication by being a 'sales congressional diplomat.'

Next, I picked my assistants from my former teachers and doctorate students from the institute, and told them. "You guys will now enter the

공부하는 국회…

16대 국회들어 의원들간에 전문분야에 대한 연구 열기가 확산되고 있다. 연구회 토론회 등 다양한 형태의 모임을 만들어 현안 파악은 물론 대안 모색에도 적극 나서는 새로운 풍속도가 자리잡는 양상이다.

이들 모임은 특히 국회 파행에도 아랑곳하지 않고 활발하게 운영돼 정쟁의 장으로 인식돼온 국회에 신선한 바람을 일으키고 있다.

◆스터디 그룹=각종 현안에 대한 의원들의 전문성을 높이기 위해 한시적으로 결성된 소그룹 공부모임. 국회파행중에도 단 한차례도 거르지 않고 모임이 계속됐다.

통일방안 연구모임에는 민주당 이종걸, 한나라당 고흥길 의원 등이 참여하고 있으며 공적자금 투명성 확보방안을 논의하기 위한 모임의 경우 한나라당 황우여 안경률 의원 등이 주도하고 있다. 또 코스닥 시장 발전방안, 전자상거래 활성화대책, 농·어민 부채경감대책 등을 논의하기 위한 모임도 순항하고 있다.

이들 모임은 홍사덕 국회부의장이 일본 의회의 '벤쿄우카이(勉强會)'라는 소규모 스터디 그룹에서 아이디어를 얻어 시작된 것. 매일 오전 7시에서 9시 사이에 3~4개 이상의 모임이 열릴 정도로 열기가 후끈하다.

홍 부의장은 "각 모임별로 토론 내용을 집약해 문제점을 개선할 수 있는 법안을 마련해 국회에 제출할 것"이라고 말했다.

◆연구회=20여개의 연구회가 결성돼 활동하고 있다. 정보통신부 장관을 지낸 민주당 남궁석 의원이

정보화시대 多알아야~
SOFA·경제현안등
전문가 초청 대안찾기

주축이 된 '지식경제연구회'는 20일 국회 파행 속에서 '지식기반경제, 어떻게 풀 것인가'라는 주제로 창립기념 심포지엄을 열었다.

민주당 허운나 의원이 이끌고 있는 '사이버정보문화연구회'도 19일 오래진 한국 CIO포럼 회장 등이 참석한 가운데 '디지털 시대의 뉴 패러다임과 정부, 기업 및 사회의 변화'라는 주제로 토론회를 열

었다. 이날 세미나에서는 원격 화상토론이 실시됐으며 연구회 홈페이지를 통해 인터넷에 생중계돼 정보화의 사각지대인 국회에 신선한 충격을 줬다.

한나라당 김만제 의원이 회장을 맡고 있는 '경제비전 21'도 18일 'IMT 2000의 올바른 사업 방향'을 주제로 토론회를 열어 사업자 선정 과정의 투명성을 높이기 위한 방안을 모색했다.

'국가보안법문제를 고민하는 의원 모임'은 18일 '국가보안법, 어떻게 할 것인가'라는 주제로 토론회를 열어 국보법 개·폐를 둘러싼 여론을 수렴했다. '평화통일포럼'도 19일 '남북경협 방안'을 주제로 토론회를 열었다.

김미리 기자
miri@hankyung.com

assembly with me. Although you will be working as my assistants, I want us to forget about that title and just work like we did at the institute. I want us to treat our job at the assembly as if we were working on another international project — with a sense of exploration and teamwork — and remember, that we're here to make a contribution to the assembly and to our country. Let's make this a very productive place. Another thing I want to stress early on is no one shall exploit his or her title for personal gains. I already know you are people of integrity and transparency, but I'm also aware that in a brand new environment, people can sometimes succumb to new temptations, so at the risk of being redundant, let this be a warning."

I also encouraged everyone to continue educating themselves, and I did this so much so that over the four years of working together, my assistants really grew a lot professionally At the end four years, they were all able land a job they were very happy with. Two of my female assistants and one male assistant decided to continue their studies and later became professors, and another assistant went on to work for another assembly member and was later recruited as an executive at Microsoft Korea.

Creating 'Wednesday Forum,' an IT Study Group for Assembly Members

Believing that we should all educate ourselves continuously, my motto became 'Studying Assembly.' Since I wanted our National Assembly to become a self-educating body, I created the 'Wednesday Forum' where all our representatives could come and learn about IT-related topics together in a study-group like environment.

The forum was held every Wednesday morning following a group breakfast. I had two goals for this forum. First, I felt that for our representatives to understand what was going on with the IT boom under the current administration, they first needed to know more about the IT field. Secondly, I thought this forum would help pass IT-related bills more efficiently and help corporations grow as well since it would help public officials, representatives, businessmen and field experts come to a better understanding of one another.

To help conduct this weekly forum, some of the members and I got together and founded the Research Society for Cyber Information Culture. The society became quite popular, and powerful congressional figures like Lee In Jae, Jung Mong Joon, Kim Jong Pil and Oh Sae Hoon all joined as well as representatives from different parties. I could tell from the high participation rate how much people had needed a medium like this to help them become educated on IT. However I must admit, I think a few of them probably just joined so they could look like 'learning representatives.'

Enacting the Charter for Cyber Information & Culture

The Research Society for Cyber Information Culture enacted the Charter for Cyber Information Culture. The charter listed things that government, corporations and citizens should follow in the internet age. On August 31, 2000, our Society held an event to distribute the charter from the National Assembly meeting room to six different locations throughout the country via video conferencing.

The event was hosted by the film actor Park Sang Won, and among the attendees were An Byung Yup, the minister of Information Communication, myself, and other representatives including Kwak Chi Young, Oh Sae Hoon, Jang Young Dal, Kim Gun Tae, Lee Mi Kyung, Kim Hee Sun, Kim Young Wha, Choi Young Hee and Park In Sang.

People from other supporting associations also attended, Park Sung Duk, director of Korean Computing Center, Park Ho Goon, head of Korea Institute of Science and Technology, Suh Sam Young, head of Korea Education and Research Information Service, Jang Moon Ho, head of Korea Institute of Science and Technology Evaluation and Planning, Cho Sun Hyung president of Girl Scouts Korea, Lee Jin Sae, head of Hyundai'

HR Research Institute, and Yoo Myung Wha, head of Korean Society for Rehabilitation for People with Disabilities. From the corporate side, Suh Pyung Won, ceo of LG Information & Communications, Hong Sung Won ceo of CISCO, Yum Jung Tae, ceo of Ssangyong Information & Communications attended the event. The events were held in Busan, Jeonju, Chunchun, Jeju, and Daejun.

The charter contained twelve fundamental propositions and was well received by media outlets that promoted healthy internet culture, such as *The Korea Economic Daily*. The first lady also sent us a congratulatory video message on the day of the event. She said,

> Hello, this is Lee Hee Ho.
>
> First of all, I'd like to congratulate the proclamation of Charter for Cyber Information Culture. I think this is very significant. The charter has been created to help realize our visions for the information and knowledge era and to iterate what the leaders of this revolution should be doing. We are living in an information age where things are changing at the speed of light, and computers are leading our time. Internet has expanded our concept of space from just the physical space to the cyber space. The cyber space is open to every person. It transcends national boundaries, ethnicity, age, sex, time and space, and is completely open. It is a place where unlimited imagination can define reality and it provides us with new dreams and challenges.
>
> However, there are difficulties some people face approaching the cyber space, and we need to be especially considerate so these patterns are not handed down to the next generations. Already, we have seen some adverse effects that should not be underestimated or ignored. The proclamation of this charter is very meaningful in this sense.
>
> I think everyone who is here today at this event has a very important role to play. I ask participants to do their best wherever they are to make sure the benefits of informatization go to all. Every one of us needs to make sure that freedom, democracy and equality are realized in the cyber space, as we all wish to see. I'd like to thank everyone who worked on this charter as well as the Research Society for Cyber Information Culture and all other civic groups. I wish everyone good health.

Movement to Make a Personal Webpage for My Fellow Representatives

Since I considered transparency as a top priority, I decided to focus on encouraging my fellow assemblymen and women to create their own personal websites. I told them, "There is no better way to show your constituents that you're a transparent politician than having your own website. You can upload your daily schedule on your webpage so they can see what you're doing. Then you won't have to distribute parliamentary reports. You could make it even more effective by adding a photo gallery to go with your different activities." I told them to look at my own website for reference since I was the only one who had one at the time. Soon, many people started making their own websites, and by 2001, every member of National Assembly had their own. The media talked about my encouragement of personal websites among assembly members and did a news coverage.

Discussing the Digital Divide with Bill Gates

One of my major accomplishments in life is no doubt starting the IPAIT (International Parliamentarians Association for IT). But before I did that, I had a chance to meet with Bill Gates. When I met him, I openly asked him for his support. I said to him, "I am trying to create an organization for international parliamentarians to come together and discuss the topic of digital divide. Our inaugural assembly is planned for next year in Seoul, and we want to talk about ways we can overcome communications protocol and establish a global standard. The problem is, many of the parliamentarians I want to invite are hesitant about coming because of travel cost. I wanted to ask if you could help us in that regard." After listening to me, he agreed that we need to work towards reducing the digital gap and told me he would pay for people who needed assistance.

Then, on the first day of our three-day inauguration assembly, he even sent us a congratulatory video message.

Creating and Being the First President of IPAIT

Following is an excerpt from *Maeil Business Newspaper*'s article 'Launching the IPAIT,' published on November 13, 2001.

> On November 13, Democratic Party's assembly woman Huh Unna, who's chairing the launch of the International Parliamentarian's Association for Information Technology (IPAIT), invited ambassadors from twenty one countries to the National Assembly to discuss its inauguration and development plan and ask each member country's government for their cooperation.
>
> At last month's meeting prior to the inauguration, Algeria and Thailand expressed their desire to host the next round of meetings for the following term. At IPAIT's inaugural assembly the following day, representative Huh was honored with the title as its first president. She said, "It's historically significant that Seoul is hosting the very first forum for politicians from all over the world to come together to reduce the global knowledge gap." She said, "I think this will reinforce Korea's international status as a powerful knowledge-based and IT-based economy."

Representative Jang Young Dal Whom I Admire

Representative Jang Young Dal was my party colleague, and he was always so supportive of all my endeavors after I began as a novice politician. Our ties go back to before my entering the political scene.

I met him while I was working on 'Women, Information & Culture 21.' He invited me as a keynote speaker at a seminar held at the assembly. He

With Bill Gates after discussing the digital divide.

was one year my senior and Korea's key democratic fighter who had spent seven years in prison for following his ideals.

That day after the seminar, he came over to me with a copy of his autobiography in his hand to give me. Published in 1999, it was titled 'Which Side Will You Be in a Battle Between Truth and Lies.'

A few days later, I was driving back to Seoul after a lecture when I found myself in a complete standstill from a heavy snowfall. The entire road looked like a parking lot with no movement at all, so I took out his book and started reading it. I started crying when I read about his fighting spirit for democracy. I thought, "He spent seven years because of what he believed in and for fighting for his country and people. After coming back from America, I've been living for my own ambitions." It made me reflect upon my own life, and I gained renewed and greater respect for him.

What made him even more admirable was that after all the hardships he went through, he was still so optimistic and free of any resentment. He was also incredibly generous and always willing to make sacrifices for others. Out of all my fellow assembly members, the ones I admire the most are Gun Tae Kim, who taught me to maintain the spirit of a democratic fighter and Mr. Jang.

1 With the members of the assembly at the Wednesday Forum.
2 IPAIT Preparations Committee with the ambassadors.
3 Greeting speech as the IPAIT president.
4 With attendees of IPAIT.

3

4

Conducting Congressional Diplomacy
All over the World

Helping Small Businesses Move Abroad
Through Sales Diplomacy

As a representative of the assembly, I also employed 'sales congressional diplomacy' in order to help smaller Korean companies in Korea move their businesses abroad. *Maeil Business Newspaper* reported on April 23, 2001 about my work in an article titled "Assembly Woman's 'Business Diplomacy'."

> Assembly woman Huh Unna of Science and Information Technology Committee has launched 'business diplomacy' to help small and medium size businesses expand their businesses abroad. On the 23rd, she flew to China to help our cyber-education businesses enter the Chinese market.
>
> After a meeting about standardization of Chinese cyber universities, she will meet with upper level officials of Hoo-Bey (湖北) to discuss having Korean companies participate in building Woohan (武漢) University's cyber university.
>
> Representative Huh also visited Sweden last month with Korean wireless internet companies. This month, she paid a visit to Mexico with audio

and video telephone companies.

She said, "Members of the assembly have the opportunities to meet with high officials from foreign countries to discuss how we can remove the obstacles that prevent our companies from moving into new markets. American politicians lobby us to send their companies to Korea all the time. Korean officials need to work on Korean business interest in conducting their diplomacy.

Representative Huh is currently visiting Mexico to help create Mexico's own version of Silicone Valley. She hopes it will become a new destination for Korean companies that are moving their businesses abroad. She is also working with Chinese Choong Bang to build apartment complexes that will house 200 million households, also hoping it will lead to more opportunities for Korean IT companies specializing in home automation and home-networking to get involved.

Visiting East Timor with a 'Friendly Delegation'

In 2003, I was chosen to lead a 'Friendly Delegation' between Korea and East Timor. In June 2003, I went and visited East Timor for a week. On our delegation, there were businessmen, international organization experts, doctors and artists. We visited the Evergreen base of Korean Peace Keeping Force and met the President Gusmao and listened to him talk about how we could help *East Timor*. He told us that he was grateful to Korea for sending our troops, and we promised them we'd give support to their medical and educational needs. President Gusmao had been a hero in the fight for his country's newly won independence and made a very strong impression on me.

Following is an article I wrote after my visit to East Timor, titled "A Representative's Business Diplomacy." It was published in the January publication of *The Digital Times*.

It has been a very busy month, and after getting back from East Timor and

동티모르(친선외교)
한-동티모르 친선사절단 단장으로

영양실조와 부실한 위생관리로 고통받는 어린아들에게 의료봉사

1

폭스 멕시코 대통령의 방문 요청

이번 멕시코 2차 방문은 멕시코 폭스 대통령의 요청에 의해 이뤄졌습니다. 2001년 4월, 허운나 의원의 1차 방문 이후 양국간 IT 협력증진 방안에 깊은 관심을 기울여온 폭스 대통령은 지난 6월 국회 방문을 통해 허운나 의원에게 그동안의 진행상황을 묻고, 구체적인 협의를 위해 다시 한번 멕시코를 방문해 줄 것을 요청하였던 것입니다.

2001년 6월 국회의장실을 방문한 빈센테 폭스 멕시코 대통령이
허운나 의원에게 멕시코에 방문해 줄 것을 요청하고 있다

2

중국 시장 개척을 위한
외교적 지원에 발벗고 나섰습니다

IT 외교로 20조원 중국 사이버 아파트 시장 공략

허운나 의원은 지난 8월 17~19일 북경을 방문, 중국 부동산개발그룹(우리나라 주택공사에 해당)이 추진 중인 '디지털 커뮤니티(사이버 아파트) 건설 프로젝트'에 우리 나라 IT업체들이 진출할 수 있도록 하는 방안을 구체적으로 협의하였습니다.

조야대 앞빌관에서 허운나의원과 중방그룹 탕호소 총재가 만나
디지털 커뮤니티 건설 프로젝트에 대해 논의하고 있다

3

1   Working as 'Friendly Delegation' in East Timor.
2   With the Mexican president.
3   On the project site for a Chinese cyber-apartment with Chairman Choong-Bang.

Mexico, I find we're already in the final week of July.

During the first week of July, I was visiting East Timor as the head of the 'Korea-East Timor Friendly Delegation.' Our delegation consisted of experts in international relations, economics, medical experts, social welfare specialists and artists. With its population of only 880 thousand people, East Timor is a small country that is still unstable, and Korean troops are dispatched as part of the UN's Peacekeeping Forces (PF) to help maintain public order. However, there are many rehabilitation projects under way.

On this particular visit, I was able to meet the country's President Gusmao. With his trademark warm smile, he expressed his gratitude for Korea's cooperation in sending its troops there and asked for our continued proactive support in the development of East Timor's economic, educational, health and medical sectors.

The president especially asked for Korea's support in advancing his country's IT sector, recognizing Korea's outstanding accomplishments in it. Some of the things we discussed included provision of computers, helping constructing an internet plaza and sending an 'Internet Youth Volunteer Group' to East Timor to teach people how to use their computers. Our Ministry of Information and Communication is in talks about these ideas, and we think many of them will take place.

In return for our willingness to help East Timor, President Gusmao seemed receptive to allowing Korea to be involved in the exploration and development of their oil and natural gas. One of the major accomplishments to come out of this visit was that as the head of the delegation, I was able to ask and receive some tangible promises from the president, such as giving Korean companies the development right for East Timor's underground resources.

If my visit to East Timor consisted of warm and friendly diplomatic work based on mutual trust, my visit to Mexico was a bit more calculated and realistic. With the Korea-Mexico FTA being on the forefront of discussions, there were many inevitably conflicting interests on both sides. The obvious advantage we had was no doubt our IT sector. We demanded that Korea and Mexico create an IT investment fund to be used in building a consortium for Korean companies that will participate in Mexico's electronic-government projects. With its ambition to lead informatizaion within the

1

2

1   At a policy meeting with a women's group.
2   On the December cover of Industrial Education, 2001.

Central/South American region, Mexico is working to create its own e-Mexico, modeled after our e-Korea and has a plan for an e-Government, which they also modeled after our own. Therefore, I think Mexico is one of the top countries Korean companies will need to pay attention to in the future.

For Korean IT companies to be able to take part in these Mexican projects will require large-scale cooperation and teamwork among government officials, assembly members, and entrepreneurs. In today's competitive world, solidarity of our entire country will be needed for Korean companies to gain a competitive edge internationally.

Not Drinking at Social Gatherings

Working as a representative, there were many occasions to attend social gatherings, and they often involved drinking alcohol. Sometimes, they were with other politicians and other times, they were with reporters. At these gatherings, people always asked me to have a drink with them, but I always declined. My life's motto is, "I can be present, but I will not drink." This isn't because I'm afraid of making a mistake or looking silly drunk. I just never learned how to drink. But because of this, many people had a wrong perception of me. Before joining the assembly, I was touring the country for my work on the educational reform committee. When I visited the countryside, the educational superintendent from the district I was visiting always brought me to the best restaurants in the area. So luckily, I had many opportun-ities to eat at some of the most exquisite restaurants all over country and taste the locally famous dishes of each place. Normally the dishes came with a matching drink, and the superintendents always wanted me to try some. Of course, I always said no. Sometimes, if they really insisted, I would fill up my glass with water and drink that instead as a gesture.

The interesting thing was, the superintendents liked to spy on each other's evaluation. One time, I learned that a superintendent from another district was spying on the evaluation so they could prepare for their own better.

Another time, I was having dinner with the executives from one of the education offices. Although they kept asking me to drink, I told them matter-of-factly that I simply didn't drink alcohol. Then one of the gentlemen said to me, "We heard you drank with the people from the other office, so how come you won't take a drink from us?" They must have been spying when I was drinking water from my glass. These tours really reminded me we need to change Korea's tradition of entertaining their guests with alcohol.

Winning with Specialty and Policy-Making Skills

Other than my 'No drinking policy,' the other policy I had was 'Avoid making statements that could stir up political strife.' Maybe this wasn't a responsible thing to do as a politician, but since I'd lived my whole life as an academic, I didn't think it would be productive for me to get caught up in a messy political conflict. As I was in the assembly as an expert in a specialized field, my job was to use my political clout to further the progress in the field of my specialty. I didn't want to turn into a political figure who was always in the middle of some controversy and fighting on television. I also identified myself more with the working class since I had built myself up from nothing, so I felt more comfortable being on the side of the people and the underdog.

There were two main stages from which members of the National Assembly spoke within the assembly. One was at each party's general meeting and the other was at the standing committee and its continuation, the parliamentary inspection. At the general meeting, party members often threw criticisms at the other party. Parliamentary inspections were usually for specialized questions aimed at government policies, budget and achievements. Nevertheless, during the election times, they were often used for political attacks, but I never used it in that way. I belonged to the Science, Technology, Information and Telecommunication Committee, and always tried to give expert opinions at the inspections. As a result, I was chosen as the top committee member each year from several NGO groups.

Introducing the World's First
Electronic Voting System in Politics

All International Eyes on Electronic Voting for the Presidential Primaries

The 16th presidential election took place on December 19, 2002 with seven candidates running for the election. The Democratic candidate Roh Moo Hyun won, defeating the Grand National Party's candidate Lee Hwe Chang.

The election marked the end of the Age of Three Kim's, and as the two candidates from the Democratic Party and the Grand National Party ran a tight competition, people watched closely to see who would win. In 2002, the Democratic Party decided to hold a public participatory primary election for their candidate. Following is an excerpt from *Maeil Business Newspaper* published on January 6, 2002.

> The Democratic Party's decision to hold a national convention marks the beginning of the first participatory primary election in the history of Korean politics. The party will begin its primary in March starting in Jeju and make sixteen stops in cities nation-wide. It plans to emulate the festive atmosphere

of the American primaries, opening up the election for everyone to join and hopefully increasing the party's support base.

They also plan on launching the world's first internet voting system where people can vote online during the months of the primaries. Results of internet voting will be counted and make up five percent of the final election results.

The cyber election which is spearheaded by assembly woman Huh Unna will have three components-an online election campaign by the candidates, cyber-voting and cyber ballot counting. One month before the primaries, each runner will launch their own site and run their campaign.

This primary was a great opportunity for me to show my capabilities as an IT expert. Because it was the first of its kind in the world, there was a lot of media attention. CNN and BBC interviewed me, and ambassadors from Australia and New Zealand visited me personally to learn about the electronic voting system.

Following is an article describing my role in the election, published in *Monthly Chosun* in January 2003.

Special Director of Democratic Party's Internet-Election

For this year's presidential election, assembly woman Huh connected the Democratic Party's candidate Roh Moo Hyun with his majority supporters — the younger voters in their 20's and 30's.

Huh's title within the election process is the party's 'Special Director of Internet Election.' With her bright and proactive personality, she has been overseeing the election plans and marketing and managing the party's website, proving just how powerful an internet election campaign can be.

"The daily foot traffic to our party's website has reached nearly 400 thousand. This is huge. I'm confident that we have secured an advantageous position over the other parties on the cyber election front."

The democrat's 'Internet Campaign Team' led by Huh has literally transformed the party's website into a second campaign site. Roh's daily campaigns are updated every evening, providing ready and easy access to voters who want to follow his move. The 'Internet TV,' which airs videos, and Singer Sin Hye Chul's program have also gained great popularity among party supporters.

月刊朝鮮 매월 1일 발행 통권 제266호 2002년 5월1일 발행 서울 중구 태평로1가 61 月刊朝鮮社(100-756) 철도특별승인 제194호
http://monthly.chosun.com

月刊 朝鮮

2002 5

민주당 대통령 후보 경선에 전자투표 도입한 민주당 許雲那 의원

사람들

민주당의 許雲那(허운나·전국구) 의원은 電子(전자)투표 방식을 도입해 민주당의 대통령 후보 선출 경선을 국민적 흥행으로 성공시켰다.

선거인단의 절반인 시민 선거인단을 모집해 「선호투표」라는 복잡한 투표방식을 도입할 수 있었던 것도 許의원이 개발한 컴퓨터 소프트웨어가 있었기 때문에 가능했다. 許의원은 「미국 같은 선진국에서도 투표 후의 개표시비 등

을 우려해 아직 공직선거에서 전자투표 시스템을 도입하지 못하고 있다」며 「전자투표 도입에 선뜻 동의할 만큼 민주당 후보자와 黨 관계자들의 「디지털 마인드」가 성숙됐다는 얘기」라고 말했다.

경기여고와 서울大 문리대를 졸업한 許의원은 한양대 교육공학과 교수를 지냈다.

사진· 李五峰 사진팀장 / 글· 金演光 차장대우

Monthly Chosun, May 2002, issue describes me as introducing the world's first electronic voting system in politics.

Working from Mutual Understanding with the President

The election committee was established in September 2002, a few months after candidate Roh won the primaries and became the presidential candidate. I was nominated as the Director of Internet Election Campaign.

But prior to all this, in June, I had gone down to an electoral district in southern Gyeonggi providence with the president (then candidate) to give a supporting speech for our party. After the first speech, we were supposed to go to the northern district for another speech. It was raining heavily that day, and as I was coming down from the stage, the president was waiting for me with an umbrella. He asked me to ride in his car together to the next stop. As we were in the car for the next two hours, we got into an in-depth conversation. During our conversation, I told him, Right now, the key word in global corporate management is 'flat organization.' Horizontal management is becoming the norm. We're moving away from the older ranks and hierarchical order system, and management is becoming more participatory. Authority is necessary, but being authoritarian isn't. Hewlett Packard has what is called the 'HP way.' Instead of standard management by objective, HP employs 'management by walking around.' If you go to their headquarter, the top level managers work in cubicles without any walls so their employees can come and see them freely whenever they need.

In Korea, if an employee or someone in a lower position submits a brief, it takes a long time for it to get to their superior and to receive an approval because of the complicated hierarchical structure. At HP, people sit close to their superiors, colleagues and subordinates, and it facilitates communication and accelerates decision-making. In Korea, to have a meeting with the president of the company is really difficult, but at HP, anyone can walk into the president's office if necessary. Within the MBWA system, any employee who has an issue can discuss it with their superior immediately. I think this is really important.

I have seen many American organizations that are horizontally structured. In the 80s, HP was the most popular company among college

노무현 대통령을

주간동아 선정 100인 … 노무현 정권 핵심인물

12월19일 밤 10시30분. 민주당사를 찾은 노무현 당선자는 두 팔을 높이 쳐들었다. TV에서는 "노무현 후보의 당선이 확실시되고 있다"는 앵커의 발표가 들려왔다. 당사는 기쁨과 환희의 도가니였다. 잠시 후 감정을 추스른 노당선자는 가시밭길을 동행한 '동지'들을 향했다. 김원기 고문, 정대철 공동선대위원장, 이해찬 기획본부장, 허운나 의원, 그리고 그외 다수 당직자 등등….

허운나 의원

49년생 서울. 경기여고 서울대 영문과 미 플로리다주립대 교육공학 박사. 한양대 교수. 영국 케임브리지대 객원교수. 16대 의원

20일 TV 생방송에 출연. 노당선자의 부인 권양숙 여사에 대해 2, 3시간씩 얘기를 풀어나갈 정도로 순발력이 있다. 권여사와도 친하다고. 노당선자가 "여성정치인 중 가장 순수하고 깨끗한 사람이다"라고 극찬할 정도로 신임이 각별하다. 이번 선거에서 인터넷 선거전을 총지휘했다.

Weekly Dong-A Magazine, January 2003, with my picture and profile under the title "100 people who made President Roh".

graduates. They pride themselves in making products of the 'highest quality,' and they don't hesitate to provide financial and technical support to small and medium companies that work with or for them. They know how to cooperate with other companies to maintain their top position. We need to get rid of our old authoritarian mentality and switch over to this horizontal structure."

It turned out that Mr. Roh shared a similar viewpoint. He resented the authoritarian way of doing things and told me if he were to become the president, he will listen to the Korean people, create a participatory government, and pursue a more balanced plan for city development through decentralization. Our preferences and visions matched nicely, and we continued with our discussion. At the end, Mr. Roh said to me, "I have spoken with many members of the assembly, but this is the most intelligent conversation I've ever had." I told him, "Since our thoughts are completely on the same page, I promise to give you my full support. I may start following you everywhere for your campaign and even bring a packed lunch."

Roh was a faithful believer that absolute power corrupted people absolutely. As soon as he came into the office, the first thing he did was reform the four most powerful political organs, which were the Prosecution, National Intelligence Service, National Tax Service and the Board of Audit and Inspection. With regards to the National Intelligence Service, he ordered it not to get mired in national politics and stated he would not accept any politically related reports from NIS.

Roh also showed his resolve by giving up his nomination right.

He'd entered politics in 1988 through a recommendation by Kim Young Sam, the president of the Reunification Democratic Party. Then he ran in the 13th election for the National Assembly in Busan's Donggu district and won. When the Reunification Democratic Party, the Democratic Justice Party and the New Democratic Republican Party all came together, he condemned the merger as an 'unethical collusion' and parted ways with Young Sam and joined the newly formed Democratic Party. In 1992, he ran again for the National Assembly but lost, and in 1998, he ran in a by-election and won. In 2000, calling for an eradication of regionalism, he gave up running in a highly favorable Jongro district and ran instead in a northern district in Busan as the New Millennium Democratic Party's candidate, but lost again. Though he was very aware of pervasive regionalism in Korea, he chose twice to run in Busan and lost both times. From this, he earned a nickname 'Silly Roh Moo Hyun.' When he finally became the president and willingly gave up his own privilege, his supporters once again called him by this name.

No Funds for
the Presidential Election Campaign Committee

After the presidential election campaign committee was established in September, it became clear that it wasn't doing its job. Roh was an unexpected candidate even within the party and lacked a solid support base. Many people within the Democratic Party couldn't hide their astonishment at his winning the candidacy.

At the time, the Democratic Party was led by Chairman Han Wha Gap, and secretary Won Gil Kim. Every time Mr. Han saw me, he would say, "The fate of this election depends on you. As the director of the internet election campaign, I am counting on you to lead us to victory." He added, "And don't worry about funding. I will come up with the money to run the campaign." Then the secretary chimed in and said to me, "Just focus on coming up with a good team. I promise I'll give you my full support." I trusted their words one hundred percent. And now, I needed money to operate my internet campaign team.

A few days after this conversation, secretary Kim fled our party and joined the Grand National Party. He was one of many who were skeptical of Roh and decided to jump ship. I had only heard of such migratory politicians, so when it actually happened before my eyes, I was beyond shocked.

Since I could no longer go to secretary Kim to discuss money matters, I went to Chairman Han and really pressed him about the issue. When asked him this time, he completely changed his tunes and told me, "Typically, it's up to the candidate to come up with his own fund." It was unbelievable.

Time was passing, and with nowhere else to turn, I went to speak with Roh himself. Since he didn't have money, his answer was, "Representative Huh, I have some youngsters who have been supporting me by doing internet-related jobs. What do you think about bringing them in to work for you?" And this is how we recruited ten people to work for our internet election campaign team. One of these guys who came to work for us was Chun Ho Sun who is currently the leader of the Democratic Justice Party.

Finally, our party's presidential election campaign headquarter was officially ready. We had Mr. Jung Dae Chul as our chairman, and directors for our eight divisions, including representative Lee Sang Su who was the secretary.

Operating the Internet Election Headquarter Has Many Costs

Despite our readiness to work, our Party provided us with zero funding. The committee could not perform its function without financial support. Out of desperation, I suggested each director should come up with ten thousand dollars from their own pockets to contribute to our funds. We finally managed to pool eighty thousand dollars, and with this money, secretary Lee finally began our campaign for the election. First, we launched a webpage for our internet election headquarter, and we also opened up 'TVRoh. com,' 'RadioRoh.com' and 'CartoonRoh. com.' We also created a girl character named 'e-Minju.' Minju was the name we gave the character as well as the name of our party (Minju means democracy).

Appealing for Help to the 'Roh Sa Mo' Group

Once our election website was running, members of the RohSaMo (meaning 'People who love Roh') began visiting the website in large numbers. On average, we were getting around 50,000 visitors each day. I thought to myself that once the daily visitors reach 500,000, this would be a sign Roh could win the election. Since we had a lot of traffic, I decided to use the website as a channel to raise our election funds. I asked people to 'donate whatever they could, even if it's just five dollars.' Then, people started sending money, and we were receiving around a thousand dollars every day. We decided to extend our marketing efforts to CartoonRoh.com.

One day, someone wrote a post on our site that said, "I'm just a regular salary earner, and this afternoon, I came out to my work colleagues about my supporting candidate Roh." After this post, more and more people started 'coming out' to support Roh, and our daily donation reached three thousand dollars. One person sent money with a touching note saying her donation came out of her savings that was going to help pay for her mother's eye surgery.

Our committee ordered me to accompany Roh on all of his campaign tours. Since he had a very hard and rigid image at the time, they wanted me to stand next to him and soften his image. My job was also to coach him about making appropriate expressions and telling him when to pause and smile during his speeches.

A Dramatic Decision to Have Roh as a Single Candidate

Within the Democratic Party, there was a strong undercurrent of mistrust in Roh's ability to beat his opponent, the Grand National Party's Lee Hwe Chang. When the National Alliance 21 party announced Jung Mong Joon as their candidate, the Democratic party fell into a panic causing a large number of migratory politicians to leave the party. Desperate, the Democratic Party came to a decision that they needed to agree on a single candidate between Roh and Jung. Each candidate now hoped to become the single candidate.

At the time, a public opinion expert Kim Heng was working as the spokesperson for the National Alliance 21 party. She and I had known each other since she was a member of my 'Women, Information & Culture 21.' As the party's spokesperson, she came up with a certain polling method that could work favorably towards Jung, and our party insisted on polls that worked better for Roh. Disagreement over how to decide single candidacy continued.

1

"나와 鄭대표가 설득하면 노사화합"

● 盧후보 PK해안선 행군

민주당 노무현(盧武鉉) 후보는 29일 영남을 다시 찾아 후보단일화 바람몰이에 나섰다. 다음달 1일까지 해안선을 따라 포항·울산·부산·마산·창원·진주·부산을 도는 2박3일간의 '영남몽' 행군이다.

노후보는 포항제철 방문후 포항 죽도시장, 울산 롯데백화점과 현대백화점 석남점앞 유세에서 "영남 몰산 노사분규 당시 (정몽준 대표를) 만났을 때는 서로 말이 안통했는데, 이제는 말이 통한다, 서로 이해가 넓어진 것 같다, 이회창 후보에게 정권 맡기기 불안해 만났더니 사람좋더라"며 鄭대표에 대해 연대감을 표시했다.

그는 "제가 노동자를 설득하고, 정 대표가 기업하는 사람들을 설득하면 노사화합도 잘될 것"이라며 "50대두 사람이 온갖 비리의혹과 지역주

포철서… 민주당 노무현 대통령후보가 29일 포항제철소를 방문, 고로를 둘러보고 있다.
포항 / 이상훈기자

의에 물든 이회창식 낡은 정치를 혁신하기 위해 마음을 모았다"고 강조했다.

노후보는 "지역주의를 뛰어넘는 '통합 대통령', 김대중정부가 아닌 노무현정부를 만들겠다"며 지지를 호소했다.

이기수기자 kslee@lkyunghyang.com

2

1 With presidential candidate Roh.
2 The Kyunghyang Daily News article from November 30, 2002, reporting the visiting Pohang Steel Company.
3 Visiting the Park Kyongni Literature Park in Wonju with candidate Roh on the first snow day of the year.
4 At a street-tent bar with candidate Roh and his support group.

3

4

One day, our committee directors were talking about polling methods. Back then, I also belonged to the camp that didn't think Roh could win, and I was only on this committee because I personally supported him and felt it was my responsibility to do the best I could to help him. In the middle of the discussion, someone suggested asking the candidate directly about what his thoughts were. So we asked Roh which method he thought was the best. His response to the question brought me nearly to tears for the second time. He said, "What do you think the public will think watching us argue over the polling method? We can't just insist on the one that works best for our team. I am willing to accept the method that the National Alliance 21 party offered."

This caused an uproar among people who understandably said, "we will lose if we follow their method." For the first time, I decided to speak up as the most junior member. I said, "Let's not resist this. We have such a great leader in front of us, so why are we so afraid? If we fight fair and we lose, so what? Then we will just be the opposing party. Let's face our opponents head on like Roh wants us to." So finally, we went with the other team's polling method, but the end result was our victory.

"Beef Up Roh's Campaign Team!"

There was already agreement that once the single candidate was chosen, the losing team would support the winning team. However, as the election date approached, Jung showed no interest in supporting Roh's campaign. Our headquarter fell into chaos. "The campaign will only be effective if Roh and Jung show up together. What are we going to do with Jung being standoff-ish like that? We need both of their wives to come and visit the local street markets too, but we can't even get Jung to show up."

One of our party advisers Mr. Kim Won Gi finally came to me and gave me a special order to deal with this situation. He said, "You should go talk to Mr. Jung and try to convince him to do something." As an alumni of

Seoul National University, Mr. Jung had been very kind to me when I entered the assembly, and people in our party thought we were close. With this order, I went to speak with Mr. Jung and told him that we needed his help asap and that we needed his wife's help too. He agreed to help, and soon, he and Roh took off on the campaign to visit the provinces.

Memories of Kim Jong Pil Grow Stronger

Kim Jong Pil and I sat side by side on the Information and Communication committee. He was nominated prime minister and was waiting for the final approval from the National Assembly. Since I sat next to the future prime minister, I was frequently photographed and shown on the newspaper those days. Sometimes, I received phone calls from reporters asking me, "What did you talk about with assemblyman Kim Jong Pil today?"

I knew Kim as a very soft-mannered and romantic politician although he was the main leader of 5 · 16 coup d'état which started the long military government phase in Korean history. He knew a lot about classic films and foreign actresses who were in them. He was easygoing and never too embarrassed to ask me questions about information communication whenever he didn't know something.

One time, I asked him, "How can one become a great leader?" Kim smiled, took out a piece of paper and wrote something on it. It said 'great fortune'(大運) in Chinese letters. Looking at it, I thought the phrase contained many meanings. I was also impressed by his fine handwriting. I still have the Chinese ink calligraphy he gave me with the Chinese idiom that says 'there is no end to a round ring.'

He was also a great mediator. Whenever disagreements with the other party's members prolonged committee meetings, he would offer to buy everyone dinner. Then everyone would say, "Hey, a senior member wants to buy us dinner. Let's wrap up the meeting."

One time, I was dining with him when he asked me if I played golf. I

1

2

1 Calligraphy writing done by Kim Jong Pil given to me as gift.
2 With Kim Jong Pil at Science and Technology Communications Committee
  meeting.

told him I didn't that I did aerobics dancing instead. I told him. "I didn't think that golf was something that professors could afford to do in terms of time and money." The next day, he sent me a full set of beautiful golf clubs. When I called him to say 'thank you,' he told me in his characteristically slow voice, "You can start practicing, and we will play on the field together in three months."

Another time, he told me, "An expert like you should serve as a minister. I will speak to the president." I was so touched. When I watch the dreary political scene these days, it reminds me more of Kim Jong Pil who could always melt the ice between the two parties with ease.

The Miracle of $100K Donation

Before the single candidate decision was reached, there was another earth-shattering incident. Our party's Kim Min Suk decided to join the National Alliance 21 party. His abandoning the party shocked me once again.

When this happened, members of the RoSaMo group rallied together in anger. Someone wrote an angry post titled, "You too Kim Min Suk?" which spread rapidly online, and these angry Ro supporters somehow managed to come up with a 100K donation. The incident of Kim leaving the party created a 'Kim Min Suk effect' causing a silent uprising on the internet.

As the number of supporters continued to rise, I too started believing we could win. Daily visitors to our website exceeded ten thousand and soon reached twenty thousand. Everyone was starting to feel hopeful.

At the height of Roh and Jung's joint campaign tour, our party advisor Kim Won Gi asked me to see him. When we met, he told me, "Since Jung doesn't have any assemblymen working for him, please go and help him out." With this order, I brought with me a fellow assembly member Kim Sung Ho and went to help Jung on his part of the campaign tour.

When we arrived at the campaign site, Jung was hard at work. At his sides, he had people who seemed like his own party members lined up next to him. As I didn't recognize any of them and felt a bit out of place, I stood quietly and watched him work on his campaign.

Towards the end of his speech, loud music came from the speakers, and Jung waved towards his audience and thanked them. He was wearing a red scarf around his neck, which was the color of his party. I, on the other hand, was wearing a yellow scarf belonging to our party. While waving at the crowd, he saw me at the back of the line. He reached his arm and pulled me toward the front next to him. I was standing alone with him on the platform now. He then took off my scarf and his, tied them together and handed me one of the ends. Both of us held each end of the tied scarves and posed, signaling our union. Reporters there must have liked this image because it was aired on the news that evening.

The next morning, as Roh and I were coming down in the elevator after a strategic meeting with the advisers, he said to me, "I thought you switched over to the other side yesterday." I didn't know what he was talking about. When we got to the first floor, our party members greeted me and said to me, "You made a great picture yesterday." Still having no idea, I asked, "What are you talking about?" They were referring to the TV news showing Jung and me holding the tied scarves together. I understood now what Roh meant, and thought to myself, "So I am criticized even when I make good a picture!" Although I tried to look at it positively, Roh's comments lingered in the back of my mind, and I felt uneasy.

An Emergency on the Last Day of Election

On the last day of campaign and the day before the presidential election, I was accompanying Jung with representative Kim Sung Ho. Roh was at another location with his team, and we were supposed to meet later in

Myeongdong and do the last joint campaign together. Afterwards, Roh would do one last round of campaigning by himself in Jongro. That was the plan.

It was decided during the election strategy meeting that morning that at the Myeogdong campaign, only Roh and Jung would go on the stage. The campaign site at Myeongdong was very crowded that day. Myself and others involved in preparation were telling other representatives about this decision and staying in one corner under the platform. But representatives Jung Dong Young and Chu Mi Ae kept insisting on going on the platform. Lee Jae Jung, who was in charge of street campaign, tried to stop them, but they didn't listen. They fought their way onto the stage, and soon there were four people on the platform. The entire plan was botched.

There were many supporters of Jung in the front row of the audience, and they were shaking a banner that said, 'Jung Mong Jun Next Time!' Clearly, these people wanted Jung to be the next president. Roh, watching these people closely, made an unexpected statement. He said, "Someone in the audience is holding a banner that says they want Jung for their next president. But not so fast. We have Chu Mi Ae, a very strong and self-confident woman who would take me by my collar and shake me if I don't lead with freshness. And what about Jung Dong Young? We also have several other contestants who are competing..." As these words came out of Roh's mouth, I instinctively looked over at Jung. He looked like a hundred emotions were going through him at once. My heart sank. There was no agreement between Roh and Jung that Roh would support Jung in the next election, but to bring up other Democratic members in front of Jung's supporters was surely going to make them sulky. He should have just said, "Of course, Jung is the best candidate for the next president!"

After the joint campaign, Jung's team all got on their campaign bus and drove to a Korean restaurant for dinner, and I went along. A big group of us all sat down at the restaurant. I was seated next to Jung, and we were expecting his wife to come shortly. The overall atmosphere was heavy, unlike at other post-campaign dinners. Then, Jung's ardent follower and a famous Korean singer Kim Heung Guk came in. With heavy breath and angry voice, Mr. Kim said, "Look at what's going on. We should have sided with Lee Hwe Chang!" Others at the table began mumbling. A little later, Jung's wife came and we started eating, and the spokesperson for the National Alliance party whispered into Jung's ear and took him outside the restaurant. As Jung stepped outside, a bunch of others followed him.

Election Committee in a State of Emergency

Tension was building as Jung's team seemed to be changing their stance the night before the election. Then, I received a phone call from one of the people who left the restaurant with Jung. He said to me, "Things are not looking good. I think Jung is really upset by what Roh said during the Myeongdong campaign. This is serious. Jung might break off. Why don't you call Roh and tell him to apologize to Jung?"

Breaking off the mutual collaboration less than twelve hours before the election would be disastrous. It would be a serious blow to Roh that could possibly cost him the election. I called Roh immediately and told his assistant to put Roh on the phone. His assistant told me Roh was still in the middle of his final street campaign. I told him it was an emergency and told him to have Roh give me a call as soon as he finished. I waited for his call for a while, and finally, I called him back. His assistant again answered and told me Roh had finished his campaign and went back to the headquarter. I told him once again to tell Roh to call me and that things weren't working in our favor right now.

After I hung up, I called our camp's adviser Kim Won Gi. When I told him what had happened that day in Myeongdong, he told me he was going to drive up to the headquarters right away. I also called Jung Dae Chul, the committee's chairman who also said he was coming down. I notified other key members about the situation and began heading to Yeoido myself.

Bad Luck Strikes the Night before Election

Before I had even arrived at the headquarter, the National Alliance 21's spokesperson had already gathered reporters and made a statement that Jung was 'withdrawing himself from the single candidacy with the Democratic party's candidate.' She explained, "We are sorry to deliver this news to the public. As candidate Jung withdraws his support for candidate Roh, we hope our citizens will make a wise decision. This evening during the joint campaign in Myeongdong, Roh made a statement that if the U.S. and North Korea were to go to war, our country would step in to stop it. Our party feels such a statement is inappropriate and goes against the spirit of mutual policy collaboration between the parties. The U.S. is our ally, and we believe there's no reason for the U.S. to fight North Korea. The single candidacy was founded on mutual policy making and respect, but Roh's statement today showed he doesn't respect these principles."

The united front had fallen. Soon, committee heads began arriving at the headquarter. By the time I had arrived, Roh was surrounded by young party members. The only person I recognized out of the group was Lim Jong Suk, but I figured Ahn Hee Jung and Lee Gwang Jae and his right hand men were also there. I spoke to Roh over the crowd. "Candidate, you need to call Jung right now and apologize. You need to fix the situation." Silence fell into the room, and suddenly, a young man looked at me and yelled, "Assembly woman Huh, why do you think we need to apologize?"

I was lost with words. I couldn't believe that they were treating me like some kind of a traitor when I had summoned the meeting to salvage the situation. Feeling strong resentment from the group, I left the room and went into the next room. Minutes later, representatives Jung Dae Chul and Kim Won Gi came in. I told these senior members about what had just happened in the other room. After hearing me, Lee Hae Chan, who was smoking his cigarette and pacing back and forth, said slowly, "No matter how high the position, if you don't want it, then you don't want it."

I pressed Kim and Jung to take an immediate action, and the two of them started pacing around. An this moment, Roh came into our room. I urged him again to apologize to Jung, and I remember my voice sounded very upset. I was somewhat expecting Roh to take my advice, but I was wrong. He looked me dead in the eye, and in an elevated voice, said to me, "Why should I have to apologize to him to become the president? If that's what it will take, I don't want to be the president!" Hearing this, I yelled back at him, "Are you trying to become the president for yourself? We want you to become the president for our country and our people. We have come this far, and it doesn't make sense for you to say now that you don't want to be the president!" This was the first time I had raised my voice since I joined the campaign. Roh then said, "I already knew Jung's true colors. What would be the point of becoming a president that collaborates with someone like that? I don't need to become a president like that." Seeing the gravity of the situation, the others all started talking Roh out of his mindset. Finally, Roh agreed to meet with Jung. Around eleven pm, Han Wha Gap and several others hastily made their way to Jung's team's headquarter.

A few hours later, the morning newspaper came out, and every single one reported 'Jung Abandons Roh' on their front page. Roh decided to go see Jung in the middle of the night at his house, but it was pointless by then. Despite Jung's party members trying to get Jung to reconcile with Roh, he refused to come out and speak with Roh.

On the morning of the election day at five am, candidate Roh called for an emergency press conference. "I am very sorry to have perturbed you so unexpectedly like this. To be very honest, I don't fully understand why this happened." Meanwhile, Jung made the statement that he 'will not vote, and (that he) will make an official statement after the election.' He then went back into hiding at his house.

Turning Misfortune into Advantage

The election day had finally arrived. Everyone had stayed up all night at the headquarter. After reporters came for the daily election briefing early in the morning, everyone went home to vote. At this point, I felt as though it was all over.

After voting, all our committee members returned to the headquarter and nervously watched the ballot count. As we watched, something astounding happened, which could only be called the 'Jung effect.' Similar to the previous 'Kim Min Suk effect,' Jung's withdrawing his support at the last minute got many young people to talk to each other sending so-called guerrilla communication on line and via cell phones, asking to rush to the ballot to cast their vote. Normally, young people don't go out to vote so much. It was a counter-rebellion. By one o'clock in the afternoon, cautious predictions of Roh's victory were being heard. Far more younger people had voted than we had anticipated, and finally, Roh was announced the winner. When the announcement was made, a million emotions went through my mind. I felt so proud to have contributed to Roh's victory as the first internet president. It was a great honor for me to watch him be elected our president.

On December 21, 2002, Korean Daily Report released an article titled, "The Age of Roh Moo Hyun, Flowering of Cyber Voter Movement."

> The entire cyber space seemed to shake when National Alliance 21's candidate Jung Mong Joon withdrew his support for the Democratic party's Roh Moo Hyun at 11 pm on the 18th, just seven hours before the election day. Within a matter of minutes, people posted tens of thousands of comments and flooded the websites of media outlets, political parties and civic organizations. Netizens' swift reaction then turned into to a concentrated campaign effort to encourage more people to participate in online-voting the following morning. This 'lightening-speed communication' also enabled thousands of Roh's supporters to gather at Gwanghwamun Gate at 6pm on the election day, rallying as 'street cheerleaders' as the ballot count began.

Changing the Geography of Korean Political Culture

This year's presidential campaign saw the Cyber Voter Movement get solidified as a form of political participation.

Professor Kim Jin Hong from Hankuk University of Foreign Studies said, "The results of this presidential election can be interpreted as a victory of Korea's younger netizens, who freely expressed their political opinions on the cyber space, over the attempts at media manipulation by certain conservative media outlets."

Last Minute Attempt to Raise Voter Participation

The impact of netizens extended over to their last minute attempt to raise voter participation. As the voter turnout remained low in the morning (AM), anxious netizens launched 'guerilla communication' online, posting instructions for each person to 'make ten calls to try to get people to vote and send text messages.'

Kim Ji Yeon, the head of social survey department at Media Research said, "Based on the exit poll, two thirds of the voters in their 50's and 60's voted in the AM, whereas over half of the younger voters in their 20's and 30's voted after 1pm.," "The younger voters' lifestyle contributed to this, but Korean netizens' last minute effort to raise voter turnout seems to have been very effective."

Korea Beats America in Having the First Internet President

On May 31, 2006, the SBS TV station hosted the 'Seoul Digital Forum 2006' at Seoul Grand Walkerhill Hotel. Communication experts from Korea and abroad attended the forum, and Google's President Eric Smidt, Disney-ABC Group's ceo Anne Sweeney each gave a special speech titled "Media's Today and Tomorrow" and "Hollywood in Seoul." All in all, there were about 2500 attendees from 60 countries, and ceo's in digital-related fields, policy makers and academics all came to discuss today's fast changing digital society and their visions for the future.

That evening, Seoul's mayor Oh Sae Hoon hosted the welcome banquet. I attended the banquet as the president of a university at the time, and I was seated at the same table as mayor Oh. The man who gave that day's keynote speech sat on my other side. This man next to me turned out to be a famous American musician and an intellectual named Will. I. Am from band *The Black Eyed Peas*. He introduced himself to me and told me his band was made up of all minorities-one black member, a woman, and a gay person. We started eating dinner and Will said to me, "In Alvin Toffler's 'Power Shift,' he said that political power will shift to the intellectuals in the future, and I think it has already shifted to the younger generation who knows how to use the internet-based multimedia. We made a song for Obama's campaign, and we're spreading it through multimedia. You wait and see. Obama is going to win." I looked at him and said, "Hey, the internet president was born in Korea first. I'm going to watch and see if the internet and multimedia will help novice Obama win the election too." As Will predicted, later that year, Obama claimed victory and became president.

Cautious Eyes Fall on Me after the Election

On December 19, 2002, candidate Roh was officially announced the winner, and crowds of people began flooding into his office. Everywhere, people were congratulating him and busy making themselves known to the new president. There were so many people around him that I couldn't get through.

The next morning when the new president elect went to the Seoul National Cemetery to pay his respects, the situation around him was just as hectic. People were swarming around, and he was escorted by security. Again, there was no way to approach him. I thought to myself, "Look at

With Jung and the Korean national soccer team's coach Guss Hiddinnk during the 2002 World Cup.

all these people. Yesterday, they didn't even believe he could win the election and kept their distance from him, and today, they're sycophants telling him how much they supported him during the election." Suddenly, I felt sad inside.

A few days later, negative criticism of me began surfacing on the internet. I was going into my room at the Assembly Member's Official Building when my assistant stopped me and told me, "Representative, there are some strange posts going around on the internet about you, so I ordered them to be deleted." I asked him what the post was about, and he told me that they were saying that I was 'part of Jung's supporters' and showing the picture of me and Jung standing side by side, which was taken at the campaign site. Immediately, I suspected it could be Roh's long time acquaintances and friends doing this as they now saw me as their competition. I thought to myself, 'I guess this is what politics looks like.' It was the moment I felt my growing pains as a novice politician.

There was a reason why Roh's young comrades were looking at me with caution. They were clearly concerned that I might snatch one of the limited secretary positions under Roh. Later, when I was seated all the way at the end of the table at the banquet thrown by the president for all party members, I realized once again I was being kept in check. I thought to myself, "Don't worry about me taking a piece of your pie. I will make my own pie!"

Being Out-Casted for Having 'Different Credentials'

Roh's people had a good reason to suspect that I belonged to Jung's camp. In their eye, my resume did not really match with Roh (who is a high school graduate, although he passed the bar exam and become a lawyer later) and matched Jung's very well. They perceived me as someone belonging to an 'aristocratic-like' higher class due to my 'elite' academic background. It made sense that they suspected me as a Trojan horse planted by Jung's

16th National Assembly Woman Huh Unna.

camp. Of course, if they actually thought about how I lost many nights' sleep trying to market Roh on the internet and support his campaign, they would have thought better, but they knew that bringing me into question would effectively alienate me from the president.

It was unfair, but there was no point protesting their behavior to their faces. I didn't want to add to this misconception either, so I purposely kept my distance from Jung after the election.

Jung was a billionaire and came from a distinctively different class than most other assembly members. On holidays, he would send his fellow representatives very expensive gifts. I had also received one of those gifts from him in the past.

But after the election, I refrained from calling him as I normally would have done to thank him for his gift. Although I knew he might have felt bad because I didn't acknowledge his kindness, I decided to keep a friendly distance from him so there was nothing I could do. Fortunately, assemblymen Kim Won Gi and Jung Dae Chul understood my position. One day, Kim said to me, "I saw the president the other day and told him that the day you went to campaign with Jung, it was me who told you to do that." Then representative Jung told me this, "I told the president that we should nominate you for a secretary position, but he didn't seem to like that you went to Gyeonggi Women's Highschool and SNU."

Running for National Assembly in a Grand National Party's Territory

After Roh became the president, two buzzwords were widely heard in the country. They were 'participation' and 'reformation.' It was obvious that the country was expecting the newly elected president and his party to deliver their promises through much needed political reformation. People were demanding changes such as more participatory elections and closing of electoral district chapters. These changes required elected officials to

Me on the cover of *Network Telecom magazine*, October 2000.

give up some of their vested power, which they've had for a long time. Soon the Democratic Party started splitting into two groups, one that wanted to hold on to the existing rights and power and the other that wanted an overhaul and a full-on reformation. The two groups battled but without a settlement. Eventually, in July 2003, those who left the Grand National Party, five people from the reform camp in our party, and the majority of people who left the Millennium Democratic Party came together and formed a new party. In October, Lee Mi Kyung and I also left the party, and joined the new one. In November, the new Uri Party supporting President Roh's reform was officially established.

For the upcoming National Assembly election, our party nominated me to be the candidate in a long-standing Grand National Party's district, Bundang. The election was going to be held in April 2004. I already knew from the very beginning winning this election was going to be a challenge due to strong regionalism.

Working as the President of ICU-Information and Communications University

The election ended with the Grand National Party's Go Heung Gil's victory. His fellow party member Park Geun Hye, the current president of the country, greatly contributed to his victory by campaiging with him in Bundang and ultimately bringing the conservative voters back together who were beginning to scatter. Then the Democratic candidate Jung Dong Young made a demeaning statement towards the elderly (he'd said during an interview, "Voters in their 60's and 70's don't need to vote. They can just rest at home.") that further exacerbated the already dire situation for the Democratic party among Bundang voters. The final vote turnout was 54.1% for Go and 40.6%. for me, followed by the Millenniums Democratic Party's Woo Kim getting 3.3% and the independent candidates Jung Gil Gang and Myung Wha Jang who got 1.2% and 0.8% each.

It was a close loss, and my party consoled me it was still a great feat I had gotten that much vote on the opponent's turf. Since even the most successful candidates from our party had only gotten about 20% of the votes in Bundang until now, I didn't feel too badly about my result. There was peace of mind in knowing I had given this my all, and I felt at ease to leave the political scene behind at last. As my grandmother always preached, I did my best and left the outcome to destiny's will.

When I went to see President Roh to say goodbye after the election, he said to me, "You worked really hard. Just wait a while and I will appoint you the minister of Information and Communication." I replied, "I really appreciate your consideration, but I'm more interested in heading a university than in being a minister." I already knew that the president's office at ICU had been vacant for the last five months. After a vote by the school's board of directors, I became its president on July 7.

1   2

3

1 Receiving the Best National Assembly's Research Society award from the
   Chairman Lee Man Sup.
2 With the mayor of Seoul, Lee Myeong Bak.
3 With first lady Mrs. Lee Hee Ho and assemblywomen and women ministers
   at the Blue House.

With President Roh after the launch of the internet broadcasting station.

Act 6

Working with Young Geniuses in Daejeon

My heart leaps up

when I behold a rainbow in the sky.

So was it when my life began

so is it now I am a man.

So be it when I shall grow old,

or let me die!

The Child is father of the Man

I could wish my days to be bound

each to each by natural piety.

— William Wordsworth, *The Rainbow*

Specialization and Globalization
Are the Key

Giving Away My Campaign Donation and
Returning to Being an Educator

I moved to the city of Daejeon, one and half hour down south of Seoul to work at ICU. As the third president of ICU, I was busy familiarizing myself with all affairs of the school. One day, my former assistants from the campaign came to see me with a bag of money. They said it was money left over from my campaign funds, which National Election Commission had kept after the campaign was over. I thought about what I should do with this money then made somewhat of an unexpected decision. Since this came from my supporters who wanted me to become a public official, I decided it should go to benefit the public.

When I went to give my inauguration greetings to the mayor of Daejeon at City Hall, the mayor, Mr. Hong, began excitedly explaining to me about the welfare program called 'Bok-Gee-Man-Du-Re' that he was working on. He told me that he came up with the idea when he was looking for an effective way to deal with all the welfare issues in different districts in Daejeon. He said the enterprise was going to provide assistance to 10,000

1

2

1 Inauguration as the president at ICU (KAIST today).
2 Conferment of degree at the 2005 ICU graduation ceremony.

households in financial difficulty, and he was looking for individuals and organizations to work with him and donate money for this business. After hearing this, I thought it was a perfect place to donate my leftover campaign fund. I told him I would make a gift of fifty thousand dollars. He seemed really surprised and asked me, "How can you donate your campaign funds to me when I'm sure you had to put in your own money to run the campaign?" I told him, "I've come back to being an educator now. By donating this money, I am reaffirming that decision to put politics behind me."

After donating that money to help Daejeon's underprivileged, there was still about 60K left in my fund. I decided I would use this money to show my appreciation to Bundang for the support I received. I told my campaign assistant, "Find out which welfare facilities in Bundang need our help," and he came up with twenty different places including orphanages, senior homes and rehabilitation centers for the disabled. I contacted the heads of these places, divided the 50K equally, and made a donation to each one. With the remaining 10K, I made a donation to *Women News* knowing they had been struggling to stay in operation and for all their work trying to expand women's rights in Korea. Finally, I had given away all the money that had ties to politics, and to me, this felt like a grand farewell party. I felt cleared of all political affiliations.

Becoming the President at the Same University I once Lectured at

Originally, ICU was a private university. It was built in 1997 through joint effort by ETRI, KT and other Korean IT businesses. With the help from the Ministry of Information and Communication, they secured the funds and built the school to advance the IT industry in Korea. The school was located within the Daedeok Science Complex in Daejeon Metropolitan City. Its aim was to produce world-class, globally competitive talents armed with complex technical and management skills to lead the Korean IT field.

At first, ICU only offered graduate courses, but in 2002, bachelor programs were added. The school only accepted 120 new incoming students each year, and about three quarter were enrolled in the engineering program while the rest were in IT management. In the graduate program, around 10% of the students were international, and in the undergraduate program, over half of the students came from foreign language high schools and special-purpose high schools. These were the most elite students of Korea. All classes were taught in English, and the school was run on trimesters, allowing possibility of finishing the bachelor's degree in three years. When I came in as the school's president, there were about 1,500 students in the entire university.

Its first president, Yang Seung Taek, believed that in order to advance our IT capability, professors needed know not only about their field but also be knowledgeable about teaching methods. Because of this, he'd asked me, then Hanyang University professor, to give training to the ICU's faculty about this topic. I agreed and brought my students from my research institute. For one week, we held a workshop for the professors at ICU. When I was inaugurated into my office as the president, many professors recognized me from my workshop and welcomed me into my new position.

Bringing Corporate Funds to Build a Joint Research Center

As the president, I believed ICU must head in the direction of specialization and globalization to become internationally competitive. Clearly, my job as the president was to usher in enough research funds so our professors could freely immerse themselves in their specialized cutting-edge research. I went to speak with Samsung Electronic's vice Chairman Mr. Lee Gi Tae who had become famous for his legendary success with Samsung's Anycall cell phone.

As an expert in wireless communication, Mr. Lee was an extraordinary manager. Back when SONY was still a leading brand, he harbored the ambition to take its place and began researching the IT field. Then years later, he achieved legendary success with Samsung's Anycall, which sold over a hundred million units world-wide and opened up a whole new era of cell phones. Mr. Lee is famous in the industry for having sent several thousand prototype phones into the incinerator because they had a minor flaw in it them. Together with ETRI and KT, Mr. Lee opened the gates to a new era of 3G cell phones, and no doubt was extremely knowledgeable about his field. He was one of the most knowledgeable ceos I've ever met, and we worked together to bring several million Samsung dollars to ICU to build a joint research center. Similarly, I also worked on other projects with KT to bring in more funds.

After I secured enough money to start the research institute, I turned my efforts to re-igniting the Start-up boom in the university. I got the funds to help the Start-up Incubating Center and began offering support to thirty Start-ups which included a few led by ICU faculty members.

I also worked on changing the existing faculty evaluation system. Faculty evaluation is not a simple concept. Depending on if it's an engineering school or a management school, the evaluation method must differ. Should those who bring in more money through their Start-up companies or those who acquire more patents receive a higher score? Or should we prioritize evaluations given to faculty by students? When it comes to these varying perspectives on achievement, there is no clear-cut answer.

Traditionally, there are three main criteria for evaluating a professor. Education, research and community service sum up the basic obligations for all faculty. The best evaluation is one that encourages and praises those who perform well across all three areas in a balanced manner. This feedback helps them to continue to improve as a professor. In the end, to make necessary changes to the evaluation method, I decided to hire a consulting firm to come up with a model.

The company interviewed our faculty, analyzed various charts and submitted their briefs. With this, I wanted to hear the opinions from the faculty themselves and synthesize a system we could all agree on. I showed the report to the professors, but everyone seemed to have a different opinion on what was best, and we couldn't agree even after several months of discussion.

Unlike a corporate ceo, a university president has limited authority over the school's HR decisions and its budget. Even if the president wants to recruit a great scholar by offering a good salary, it often gets thwarted because of the budget limit. When I was the president, I wanted to bring in more scholars from abroad to stir up competition in the existing faculty and motivate them to work harder, but the budget was often a problem.

Focusing Greatly on Students' Character Development

The next challenge I faced as the president was how to help our students to develop a strong character. ICU was clearly full of bright and extremely talented students who attended university on full scholarship. But because of their workload, they led a very repetitive life, moving back and forth between their dorm room and the lecture halls. Often, their only entertainment was playing computer games. There was very little romance in their daily campus lives, unlike in my undergraduate days. I couldn't let our campus stay so dreary.

I saw that things needed to change, beginning with a gym and other facilities where students could enjoy sports and physical activities. We built an inline skating rink, a basketball court, a volleyball court, and a rock-climbing wall. Even the annual school festival was a bit dry at our university, so we decided to invite some famous singers to spice it up. But despite these efforts, our students still seemed emotionally stiff. While I was the president, ICU lost one student from suicide, which was a huge shock to me. I asked myself why such tragedies happened, and I realized there were some serious problems within the education system in Korea.

I saw our students were being raised from young age as test-taking machines, and this culture and the pressure they faced pushed them to sometimes make an extreme choice when they didn't get the grades they wanted.

I thought these were tragedies that came from not knowing the real meaning and value of life. This was something that I as an educator had to reflect upon and do something about. I decided a special program was needed to help our students develop emotionally and socially. I hired a Harvard graduate woman professor to be a student counselor who would listen to their inner problems. Of course, I knew this issue was deeper and going to take more than just student counseling. I also felt that the professors needed to be more actively involved in helping their students develop as a person. I asked each faculty to take on the mentor role for their students and fostered a one-on-one mentor-student relationship at school.

I knew that lot of the emotional issues our students were having came from their earlier years. Though these measures had their limits, they were the first steps in trying to provide better guidance to our students, and personally, it felt good to know that I'd done the best I could to address this problem.

Daejeon into the World, and World into Daejeon

Korea Can Be a Mentor to Developing Countries

In order to globalize ICU, I needed to know where Korea stood internationally with regards to IT technology. It turned out, Korea was ready to seize global leadership in IT and even be a role model for developing countries in the Middle East, Africa, South America and Central Asia. These countries were far behind in terms of their technology but had enormous natural resources. This made me think, "Korea's future may well depend on their resources. Korea being an export-oriented country, these countries are also our market and a future place of employment for our students. We need to bring these countries to our side so we can gain their resources and acquire their market before others do. How can I do this?"

At this time, President Roh was making a lot of visits to these countries. So right after his visits, I flew out to the same countries and offered scholarships to promising young students and future leaders to bring them to ICU. Then, I went to see the prime Minister Lee Hae Chan and told him, "I have an idea. I'd like to go to all the developing countries the president has visited and recruit a large number of their future leaders to ICU. As they study in Korea, they will become pro-Korean just like I had become pro-American and consider it my mentor country after studying there. I think it's time for Korea to become a mentor country too. We need to bring in and educate foreign graduate and PhD students. When they return home after their studies, they will fill various leadership positions in their country, which will benefit Korea's interests. We need these bright students to come to Korea, and we need scholarships to attract them. I can't do this just with our university budget. Can you help us using the ODA (Overseas Development Assistance) funds? We will use that money to recruit foreign talent."

Thankfully, Prime Minister Lee agreed to spend a large amount of that fund for ICU. With this money, we created the Information and Telecommunication Technology Program (ITTP) at the school, which is still in place now at KAIST (ICU was merged into KAIST, which I'll talk about later). Presently, there are students from over 50 countries in the world who are enrolled in the program.

Recruiting Talents from Resource-Rich Countries

Once we received the funds and ITTP was established, I began the recruitment process full on. I chose Saudi Arabia, Oman, Qatar, the UAE, Algeria, Chile, Mexico, Brazil, Azerbaijan, Uzbekistan, Kazakhstan, Turkey and Lithuania as my main destinations, since they were all rich in natural resources.

I had imagined something like a business transaction between Korea and these countries, which could be described as an 'educational aid.' Of course, countries like Saudi Arabia and Qatar were rich oil countries that didn't need Korea's help at all, but our superior IT skills were a valuable asset they still desperately needed. Thankfully, my political experience was helpful in my negotiations with these countries. Before flying to each country, I contacted the Korean embassy there and asked for their recommendation on possible candidates to recruit. Then I would fly out, meet with the ambassador privately and decide on the finalists for selection. I also visited the universities and workplaces of these students personally.

Exporting Video Education
to Sultan Qaboos University in Oman

When I was visiting the Middle Eastern countries, I learned that though they were rich from their oil, they were lacking in human resources. As a result, there were many foreigners who served in university positions in these countries. Each time I visited one of their universities, their officials would tell me to "please send some Korean IT professors here."

One time, I was visiting Oman and had just landed at the Muscat Airport. When I arrived, the president of the Sultan Qaboos University picked me up in his luxury BMW. For the next two days, he personally showed me around beautiful natural sites, castles, and we even went to the world's second largest mosque. He then asked me if I could please send some Korean professors to his university. Since ICU didn't have enough professors to send to Oman, I suggested having a real time video-conference lecture between ICU and his university. From this convert-sation, we came up with the 'ICU-Sultan Qaboos Remote Education Program' which consisted of real time video class lectures. The president was so passionate about education he later visited ICU twice and showed great interest in the lecture model ICU had developed. This was the first time we had ever exported an online Korean educational program to a country in the Middle East. Later, when I visited Oman again, I was able to meet their minster of Information and Communication through the Korean ambassador. Before this deal with Sultan Qaboos University, Oman to me was just a country in a corner of the Middle East, but after getting to know this passionate and kind university president, Oman left a very positive impression on me and touched my heart.

King Saud University Is Off-Limits to Women

After working with Sultan Qaboos University, we tried to make our way to King Saud University. This is when I found out that my entry to Saudi Arabia had suddenly been denied because I was a female. Originally, the school had assumed that a Korean university president visiting them was a man, but when they found out otherwise, they changed their mind. I couldn't understand, but since there was nothing I could do, I decided to return to Korea.

After I came back to Korea, the Saudi minister of education who had heard about my visit to Oman came to visit ICU. I told him about my denied entrance to Saudi Arabia, and he told me he would take care of the problem this time and that I should come. Shortly after, I received a formal invitation from the Saudi government and was able to fly over there successfully and pass through immigration.

King Saud University was an enormous school with close to 75,000 students. When I met with its president, I had to ask him, "Our ICU's student body is only a tiny fraction of yours. How can we give you any help?" He replied, "Yes, your school is small in size, but you have outstanding brainpower in your students." Apart from the main campus, the university had several other campuses. I learned that only male students could study on the main campus while female students were on the other. The president wanted me to help improve the curriculum at the other campuses where female students attended. I gladly accepted his request.

The campus we visited was about thirty minutes away by car from the main campus. The university officials drove me there, dropped me off at the front gate and asked me to walk in by myself. It turned out they couldn't

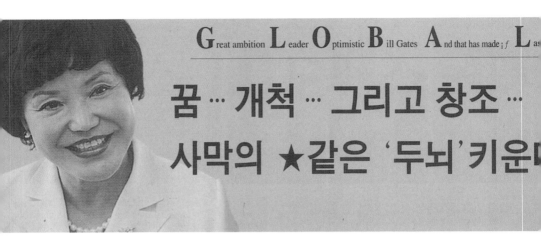

G reat ambition L eader O ptimistic B ill Gates A nd that has made ¡ f L a

꿈 … 개척 … 그리고 창조 …

사막의 ★같은 '두뇌' 키운다

Herald Economy, September 15, 2006 introduced me as a global IT leader.

enter because they were men. I couldn't believe this, but I followed the rule and went alone.

Interestingly, I noticed that the students on campus were walking around dressed freely, whereas the women I saw outside the campus all had their black robes and covered their faces with a hijab. This was a space that belonged only to women, the complete opposite of the main campus.

All their female professors had been educated and received their degrees from either the U.S. or Europe. They represented the intellectual elites of this country. I said "hello" to the professors, and they all asked me looking serious, "Did you already visit the main campus?" I told them I had, and they said no one from their group of faculty had been there so they were envious. I realized the irony of this and also how closed off and backward these rules were. I suspect I was probably the only woman who's ever walked on King Saud University's main campus dressed in regular clothes with my face uncovered.

Receiving the So Called 'Indian Nobel Prize,' the Priyadarshni Award

As I traveled the world and visited many countries trying to export Korea's IT skills and reduce the global knowledge gap, I was given the honor of receiving the Priyadarshni Award, the so called 'Indian Nobel Prize.' Following is an article from *Korean Daily Report* featured on September 20, 2006, with a title "Huh Unna, president of ICU, receives the Priyadarshni Award."

> On the 19th, ICU's President Huh Unna received the 22nd Global Priya-darshni award for IT Education at the Hilton Hotel in Mumbai, India.
> The Priyadarshni award was created in 1985 and is an internationally renowned prestigious award. It is often considered the Indian equivalent of the Nobel Prize. President Huh is the first Korean to have received the award.

With India's minister of Industry after accepting the Priyadarshni Award.

At this year's ceremony, there were twelve award winners, including Narayana Murthy, the chairman of a global IT corporation Infosys and chairman Toru Hasegawa of Yamaha.

The awards are given out by India's largest NGO, Priyadarshni Academy, to individuals who have made substantial contribution to the international community and humanity in twelve different sectors: Education, Culture, Science, Medicine, Environment, Human Rights and International Cooperation.

The foreman of the jury Ram Tanejee said they chose President Huh because "by recruiting promising young talents from comparatively weaker IT countries and bringing them to Korea, she transferred policy know-how's and first-hand experience with cutting edge IT technologies and helped advance the global IT education and reduce the knowledge gap."

A True Intellectual Is Not Prejudiced

When I was running the ITTP program for foreign graduate and doctorate students, I came to think deeply about what makes someone a true intellectual.

There were many Muslim students in the ITTP program. Because Muslim people pray several times throughout the day, I decided to build a prayer room on campus for them. This incited an angry response from one of the Korean students. The student wrote a post on the school's website complaining that it was unfair the school didn't provide a prayer room for its Christian or Buddhist students. This seemed childish and unreasonable to me since there were many churches and Buddhist temples everywhere in Korea, which was not the case for mosques. So I decided to ignore the post.

Then, I found out some of the university employees were not happy that ITTP students received full scholarships to study. They complained that since ICU didn't have enough money to hand out scholarships to its own

1   With university presidents from abroad.
2   Delivering the keynote speech at University President Forum.
3   With ministers of IT from various countries.
4   Hosting the SBS Seoul Digital Forum.

students, it shouldn't be offering scholarships to foreign students. These two incidents made me think about what attitude I should embrace as an educator and an intellectual.

I believe being an intellectual isn't defined by a person's graduate or doctorate degree alone. In my opinion, you need to be free from prejudice and other preconceived notions. No matter how much knowledge you have, if you can't open your mind to embrace ideas and opinions that are different from what you have previously known - if you can't be flexible in the way you think - you can't become a true intellectual. For me, personal growth means embracing diversity, and in general, I think Korean people still need to learn to be more open to other cultures and more understanding towards them. We need to become more 'culturally intelligent and sensitive.'

The Brazilian Ambassador Approves of ICU's Foreigner Degree Program

Today, even though ICU has been incorporated into KAIST, ITTP continues on, and the labor I poured into the program seems to be paying off.

These days, I am working as an advisor at Chadwick School in Songdo. One day, the school's Brazilian admissions director came to see me and asked me if I knew a Brazilian man named Daniel Fink. I told him I didn't, and he said, "Daniel is the first secretary to the Brazilian ambassador to Korea and he's an ITTP graduate. He told me he had many fond memories of you." The two had met at a Brazilian expat meeting in Korea.

Then a few weeks later, the ambassador invited both of us to a dinner at the embassy. He told me, "Our embassy's first secretary raved to us about his positive experience at ITTP. He said we should spend our own money to send more students to study in that program, so I'm going to tell our government about sending more students to ICU. Congratulations for building such an excellent program."

Soon after this conversation, Daniel brought several ITTP graduates who were working in various sectors in Korea and twenty current students to Songdo to see me. This was such a proud, touching moment. Korea had become their mentor country as I had imagined, and I was like a maternal figure in their mind.

Launching the International Forum for Presidents on Information and Communication Technology

If ITTP was one of the major pillars for globalization of ICU, the other pillar was the IFUP, launched in Daejeon in October 2006. Distinguished university presidents from all over the world gathered together in Daeduck under the banner of 'Training the IT workforce of the 21st Century: IT talents global corporations want.' Among the keynote speakers were Mr. Kothari, the former president of ITT, Alan Eustace, a publisher of nine books and ten patents in micro-processor chip design, and the chief vice president of Google.

MIT Professor Nicholas Negro Ponte was scheduled to deliver the keynote speech but was unable to make it to the event on time due to a terror alert at his departure airport in London. However, when he finally did make it to the event after three flight transfers, he received the audience's fervent applause.

On the first day of the forum, Bill Gates sent a video message. He said, "Over the last ten years, we have achieved so much through our technological revolution. The next ten years, we have to train new man power through our mutual cooperation." "We need a lot more innovators for future technology. I welcome and applaud the launching of this forum and hope it will produce the kind of IT talents we need.

A Veteran Doesn't Die
but Just Moves Backstage

Political Community Questions ICU's Identity

Now comes the heartbreaking story of how ICU was integrated into KAIST. ICU was originally built with the Informatization Promotion Fund from the government to produce top IT talents. Initially, they wanted ICU to be a public university, directly under the Ministry of Information and Communication. But due to opposition by the Ministry of Education, it became a private institution. However, the minister of Information and Communication was the chairman of school's board and brought government support and supervision to the school. ICU had already been in place for ten years when I became the president. But when I took office, the political community began to stir up controversy and question the school's legitimacy.

This was led by Kim Young Sun, an assembly woman from the Grand National Party. She was on the Science, Technology, Information and Telecommunication Committee during the same time that I was and was similarly one of the star women members of their party. She argued that ICU should not receive money from the government since it was a private institution. She advocated that ICU should be integrated into KAIST if it continued to receive government support. The Ministry of Information and Communication saw this coming and tried to turn ICU into a public school with help from a special bill. Unfortunately, the bill got stuck in the assembly and was thwarted. Representative Kim was determined to bring ICU down, and rumors circulated in the political community that she was envious of me and trying to sabotage my work.

The *Joongdo Ilbo* the political battle surrounding ICU in their October 22, 2004 issue.

> As the controversy surrouding the legitimacy of ICU's original founding continues, a great deal of struggle is forecasted before ICU's special bill can pass the National Assembly.
>
> At the general inspection held by the Ministry of Information and Communication on the 21st, Grand National Party's representatives from Science, Technology, Information and Telecommunication Committee casted their vote against the university's special bill.
>
> Members of the Grand National Party are arguing that Information Promotion Fund has been wrongly used to create the university. However, ICU is headed by the former Uri Party's assembly woman Huh Unna, and there is speculation that political motives also play a part in their staunch opposition.

Nobody had predicted Roh would become the president over Lee Hui Chang, the presidential candidate of Grand National Party. Kim had been much favored by Lee, and had Lee won, she would have most likely been chosen as the minister of Information and Communication. Roh becoming the president had quashed that dream, so it made sense that my being the head of a university directly under the ministry did not sit well with her. Of course, all of this was media speculation, and I didn't discuss it publicly with anyone. In the past, she and I had been on quite friendly terms. Once we were both invited to Japan by the Japanese government as part of the '10 promising Korean leaders.' I was chosen as the female member of my party and she was chosen as the female member of hers, and we had a fun trip together. So it came as a big surprise that she would now take such an aggressively offensive stance towards ICU. My response to this was firm and absolute. I said ICU should absolutely not be integrated into KAIST. Though it was a small school, ICU was doing extremely well on its own and deserved to stay independent to become a world-class IT school. The fact that ICU had 100% employment rate for its graduates was a proof of this.

"ICU Cannot Be Integrated into KAIST"

My response to representative Kim Young Sun's demand for ICU's integration into KAIST was a firm and resounding "No." My reasons against integration are illustrated in one of the interviews I did. Below is an article titled "ICU's President Huh Unna, Producing IT Talents. 100% Employment Rate for Six Straight Years," which appeared in the January 6, 2005 issue of *The Financial News*.

> There is an air of vitality at Korea's only first-class IT-focused educational institution, ICU. Since its founding in 1999, ICU has seen 100% employment rate for its graduates, and it continues to be active in its collaborative work with other distinguished universities abroad. Over the years, ICU's reputation has been steadily rising, and it now attracts many talented international students who come to Korea to study there. A lot of this progress can be attributed to the work done by the university's President Huh Unna. President Huh said, "My ultimate goal is to turn ICU into a training ground. We want to produce top IT talents who will be globally desirable." She continued, "I want to make sure our graduates are so well equipped by the time they graduate that international IT corporations like MS, Oracle and HP will compete to scout them." She added, "I am working hard to see that ICU becomes one of the top ten universities in the world over the next ten years."

President Roh visiting ICU and receiving a brief.

Asking For Support from the Prime Minister

With the school under continued attack and being labelled 'illegal,' I put up a strong fight pointing out that it was 100% legally established by the National Assembly itself. Still, I needed more support, so I went to see the Prime Minister Lee Hae Chan. After hearing my plea for help, he summoned the ministers of Education, Science and Technology, Information and Communication, and asked them to come up with a plan to protect ICU. Unfortunately, representative Kim was persistent and unwilling to let the issue go, and all of the help from the ministers failed to save the school. Although Kim was pretty, she was quite aggressive and strong, and even the ministers didn't know how to handle her. While all the efforts were proving feeble, President Roh himself came down to visit ICU. I wanted to talk to him and explain all the reasons ICU should remain the way it was, but right before his visit, the minister of Information and Communication asked me not to discuss the issue with the president. He promised they would find a solution somehow. I fully trusted this promise, but looking back, I may have been a bit naive to do that.

KAIST's President Eyes ICU

Kim and her political circle continued their relentless attack demanding ICU's integration with KAIST. Then in the midst of this political campaign, a new president took office at KAIST in June 2006. After taking his office, President Nam Pyo Suh immediately began eyeing ICU for its vast land, funding and faculty. Apart from its main Daejeon campus, ICU also had a second campus in Seoul. President Suh quickly joined assemblywoman Kim and other influential members of the committee, visiting the cabinet office himself and making it very clear his intention was to expand KAIST's current funding by taking over ICU. The cabinet office was torn. It had received orders from the prime minister to protect

ICU. In December 2006, the office held a meeting to reach a compromise between the two sides. At the meeting, President Suh insisted that by integrating with ICU, KAIST could finally become world's top 10 universities.

On December 15, 2006, *The Digital Times* reported, "Will KAIST and ICU be Integrated or Will Status-Quo be Remained?"

> Government departments sat down at a negotiation table to mediate the diverging opinions about the ICU-KAIST integration. The closed meetings were held in the Cabinet Office on the 12th attended by Seo Nam Pyo, the president of KAIST, Huh Unna, the president of ICU and the vice ministers of three ministries; Ministry of Information and Communication, Ministry of Education and Human Resources Development and Ministry of Sciene and Technology.
>
> ICU stood firmly against integration, arguing that its emerging success meant integration with KAIST would result in reduced competitiveness for both universities. In reponse, KAIST representatives argued that integration of ICU's highly competitive IT-related departments would propel KAIST to become globally competitive.
>
> The meeting did not end in an agreement by the different ministries involved in the discussion, and the final decision will have to be made by the prime minister after going through the mediation process.

ICU Is Finally Integrated into KAIST

As the battle gained momentum, opinions began to shift in students and faculty. Those who were originally adamantly opposed to integration started changing their minds and said, "Maybe a diploma from KAIST would be more helpful than a diploma from ICU" and "It might be better to be a KAIST professor than an ICU professor."

The final decision belonged to ICU's board of directors. They were the ones who built the school, and fortunately, they were very much against

ICU's integration. Only the minister of Information and Communication stood with the other side because of the constant berating from Kim. Since I knew Minister Noh Joon Hyung very well, I spoke to him personally and asked him not to pass the bill that would force the integration. He told me in exasperation that the committee was refusing to approve the Ministry's budget unless he agreed to ICU's integration. Out of options, I decided to talk to the president as my last resort and let him know how unfair this would be to ICU. Thankfully, the president ordered Blue House policy director Byun Yang Gyun to make sure ICU stayed intact. I was relieved and hopeful that finally things would be settled the right way. Then out of nowhere, scandal of the year broke in September of 2007, which involved Byun and his mistress, and he was ousted overnight.

His successor was Sung Gyung Reung, a former university professor who had served on the Balanced National Development Committee. When I went to meet him, he confessed to me that all the ministers had already made up their minds and there was nothing he could do at this point. As all of this was happening, the minister of Information and Communication resigned and a new Minister Yoo Young Hwan came on, and he began preparing for a board meeting to make a final decision for ICU. Representative Kim also threatened Yoo that the ministry won't get their budget passed unless they integrated ICU to KAIST. The minister contacted each board member and convinced them to vote for integration. During the negotiation process, he also offered me the president position at KAIST's branch campus, which I declined. I had already submitted my resignation letter at a meeting we had before the final board meeting.

Then, at the final meeting, I really spoke up as I was fighting my last battle at war. None of the board members said a word in response, perhaps out of embarrassment for having betrayed their own conviction. They also requested the meeting stay private with no recording. I agreed to their terms but asked my part of the meeting to be recorded. I wanted to make sure all the injustices regarding the political sacrifice of this top IT university was going to be on record. After I finished speaking, there was complete silence in the room for several minutes. I felt like everyone knew in their heart what was happening to ICU was not right, and my speech made them feel ashamed of their own decision.

Below is an article published on November 21, 2007 in *The Seoul Newspaper* titled "ICU-KAIST Integration a Misfortune for IT Industry."

> ICU's President Huh Unna said on the 20th, "The forced integration of ICU into KAIST egged by Ministry of Information and Communication is irresponsible, and it's a huge misfortune for Korea's IT industry."
>
> At the press conference held at ICU, President Huh said, "The issue of integration should have been discussed objectively and approached with a view towards developing Korea's IT industry. Instead, the ministry is using their budget for the next year as a collateral and pressuring ICU's board of directors to agree with integration, when the fact is these two schools are clearly different in their goals and their nature."
>
> She continued, "I will continue to stand by my conviction and oppose ICU's integration. There is a board meeting tomorrow, and if they decide on the integration, I will resign my post as the president." Huh has already submitted her resignation at the last board meeting.
>
> She stressed, "Korea's only IT university is on the verge of closing down. It's been caught up in a wasteful political discourse, and it's dealing with a lack of accountability from the Ministry of Information and Communication. Instead of closing ICU down, government should provide it with policy and funding support until it can stand on its own. It should allow ICU to operate freely and give it access to the existing development fund (of 100 million won) to help maximize its profit."

Despite my plea to the government, the National Assembly and the Blue House to save it, ICU was integrated with KAIST at last. Political strife had brought to ashes ICU's visions to produce Korea's top IT talents. What could I say? Life didn't always flow in the direction of right. I did my best to stop it, but I wasn't strong enough to stop the wheels of history from turning as they did.

@ICU 2007 IT Policy Program for Senior Officials

1 High officials from around the world attending an IT Policy Program hosted by ICU.

2 Me with students from ICU's Global ITTP program.

1

2

3

1 At the International Forum for University Presidents (IFUP) hosted by ICU.
   With Dr. Negroponte and President Park Chan Mo.
2 At IFUP with UAE's HCT Centil Nathan and China's BIPT Jin Tong Lin.
3 Me giving a keynote speech at the forum.
4 Signing an MOU with the president of University of South Australia, Denise
   Bradley.
5 With Alan Eustace, Google's vice president.
6 With Mr. Eustace and the Prime Minister Jin Dae Jae at the forum.

4

5

6

1

2

3

1 Signing an MOU with the Lithuanian government.
2 With Lithuanian vice minister of Transportation and Communication.
3 Signing an MOU with Algerian minister of Land Development and Environment.
4 Visiting UAE's minister of Higher Education Mr. Nahayan.
5 Signing an MOU with president of Sultan Kaboos' University, OMAN.
6 With the president of Qatar University.

4

5

6

Act 7

You Need a Comma in Life

Beauty is truth, truth beauty.

That is all ye know on earth,

and all ye need to know.

— John Keats, *Ode on a Grecian Urn*

Good Times with Good People

Finally Having a Break at 60

I've had a busy life. At forty years old, I was on a sabbatical in Cambridge and at fifty, I got to spend time at Motorola University in the States. Now, I was sixty, and after my resignation, I got to take another break year. I had always been moving forward at a very fast pace, and it was time to stop and take a breather. Looking in the mirror, I told myself, "Korea went through a brutal war and transformed itself from a dirt poor country to a developed one in a half century. You went through something similar, with the years compressed and lived to the full. You talk fast, walk fast and act fast, and you could do so much more work because of that. You've been called the best and the first at your university, at the National Assembly, and again at a university. You've had the honor of helping to turn a new page in Korea's history. You've accomplished your goals pretty well, so shouldn't you be satisfied? Isn't this enough? You are a really lucky person. Many people have the will and the ability, but not the luck. But you did everything you ever wanted. Aren't you thankful for all of this? The wheels that had been racing forward have suddenly stopped, and now you're feeling a little confused. But, in retrospect, doesn't the weight of the past years seem peaceful and quiet now? I think it's time to really enjoy some relaxing time."

One thing I have always admired about western people was their ability to maintain clear boundaries between work and rest. So I decided to truly enjoy this time and relax. I wanted to stay away from any kind of work that I had done in the past.

Still, relaxation didn't mean I was going to stay home all day. I wanted to try and do the things I had always wanted to do but didn't have the time for. The first thing that came to mind was dancing. When I was a young girl, I did traditional Korean dance. After I had my first child and moved to Washington D.C., I took aerobics class. Aerobics was something I had done since 1978. I decided to step it up and try a real dance class this time. I found myself a dance teacher to teach me Waltz and Tango.

I also needed to change my work-centric living pattern. I realized just how much of my life had been revolving around work and professional goals. I decided to form new relationships that had no real objective and be more attentive and communicative with my friends and acquaintances than before.

Meeting with My Students from Hanyang: Huh-She and Huh-Dang

I had stayed close with some of the students from the institute at Hanyang after I'd left. I used to invite them to parties at my house a few times a year; and after I left the school, we still met on my birthday to celebrate together. These students had gone on to become socially established and family-oriented; and they were now growing old with me. In the beginning, they were young students, but over the years, my students were bringing their children to my parties, an indication that I had reached the age of having grandchildren and being a grandma.

When I was on my sabbatical at Motorola University, one of my students Um Woo Young came to visit me with his young son, and later, it was amazing to see that this little boy had now grown up, entered high school and become an awesome student.

My students and I began meeting up more now that I was free, and they came up with the name 'Huh-Dang' for our group, which means 'Huh's Party'(Dang means 'political party'). Then the girls from this group formed a smaller group on their own and called themselves 'Huh-She' which meant all the she's that followed her, which was me.

There were a lot of professors in the Huh-She group and a lot of ceo's in Huh-Dang. Some of my proteges would say to me, "Our industry projects at the institute sustained us. We learned the entrepreneurial spirit from you, and when we went into the real world to do the kind of things you were doing back then, we realized what it really took." Their words of affirmation really made me the happy. My lovely students would say to me, "Meeting you has changed my life," "I received the scholar and entrepreneurial gene from you," "You gave us motivation and inspiration," "You are my role model." Of course they were being overly kind, but it's true that my teaching philosophy has always been to give inspiration to my students and help them utilize their full potential.

Each year, about thirty students from Huh-Dang gather to celebrate my birthday. We also started meeting on Memorial Day for a golf tournament and just had our second annual game this year. Since nearly all of my students are very busy, Memorial Day is the only day that everyone is free.

I always tell my students, "If it will benefit you, you can always use my name. I believe teachers should be like a fertilizer for their students. The fact that you are my students may open a lot of doors and facilitate your lives in this country. If you need a letter of recommendation, you can ask me anytime. Dr. Morgan was my fertilizer, and I want to be yours."

The Huh Sa Mo Group

Another group I met with was called Huh Sa Mo, which meant 'people who love Huh.' This group was made up of Korea's top female leaders who all supported each other. The group had another name for it 'Rainbow' because the seven key members of the group were all unique individuals like colors of the rainbow. We came up with the name spontaneously on one autumn day when we were riding a cable car and admiring the beautiful autumn sights on a mountain near KT's Yong Pyeong training Center.

Most group members are leaders in the ICT (Information and Communication Technology) field. Dr. Song Jung Hee is the first member. After working for Samsung and being a project manager at the Ministry of Information and Communication, she is now the vice president at KT. She is very pretty, smart and one of the most amazing female figures in Korea. During her time as the project manager, she helped the Minister Jin conduct national projects and manage IT companies. She also helped the mayor of Seoul Oh Sae Hoon as Seoul's CIO and was eventually selected by KT's chairman for the highest position in the company ever reached by a woman. I used to talk with her a lot about work, and she has always proved to be a person of integrity and honesty. She is definitely the pillar of our group.

I met ceo Bae Hee Sook one year at an international conference where I hosted a panel of government ministers and vice ministers in English. She came up to me later to compliment me, telling me I was the pride of Korea, and that was our very first conversation. For the next 15 years, she remained a very close, loyal friend. She is unique and has great leadership as a female ceo. I have watched her grow so much over the years. She courageously jumped into the IT field even though she wasn't an expert, created a company that was based in high tech, and served twice as the president of Women's Venture Organization. A true woman warrior and a dear friend, I suspect she and I may have been lovers in some past lives.

KT's execute director Lee Young Hee is the first female execute member at KT. When I was working at the assembly, I complained to KT's ceo concerning the absence of women executives there. After that conversation he picked her as the first one, and then raved to me about how fantastic she was. She helped me a lot during my assembly days. When she was working in China as the overseas president, she was always there to help me whenever I visited China. She speaks Chinese beautifully and, after she returned to Korea, was promoted to executive director in charge of overseas business. An extremely busy woman, she is like salt to the group, an essential ingredient.

Executive director Lim Soo Gyung and I met when I was the co-chair of RFID and she was the director at LG CNS. She was that archetypal strong working woman, standing equal next to her male colleagues in a very male-dominated company. She always greeted me with a smile, and I was mesmerized by her soft face and clear skin with a pleasant smile. Later, she became the first female CIO at National Tax Service and then became the executive director at KT. She is a social lubricator who always brings laughter to the group.

Director Park Nam Hee is the biggest fashionista in the group. Now in her fifties, she still maintains a girlish figure, and she always wows us with her fashion sense. She worked for a long time as a director at MS and just recently quit to start the next new chapter of her life as a jewelry designer in Rome, Italy. She was the floor leader of our group, always providing entertainment, and also the mascot for the group. We hope to have a spontaneous reunion in Rome soon.

Yoon Gyung Hee is my junior alumna whom I consider one of my students because she worked with my institute at Hanyang when she was in university at Ewha. We later rekindled our friendship when her husband went to FSU to study and both she and her husband got their PhD in Education Technology. Our friendship became deeper after I selected her husband to work at Hanyang as a professor. Ms. Yoon worked for a long time at Samsung SDS and is not only a competent professional, but she also has a great sense of humor and a charming demeanor that draws people to her. She is truly a lovely person who is both like a little sister

I want to look after and a friend I want to lean on. These days, she heads a new business she began.

Executive director Oh Sae Hyun is a modern beauty who is tall and very attractive with a sexy figure to match. She also has a degree from Germany and is the sister of Seoul's mayor. She started working at an IT-security company and later, she was chosen by KT's president as executive director to bring fresh new ideas to the company's new business ventures. She is the cutie of the group.

Executive director Yoon Sim is the hottest 'It' woman leader in Korea these days and was recently promoted at Samsung SDS as the executive director. She has real talent and dedication to match and is a super-mom who manages her work and home life beautifully. She also hosted a fabulous promotion party at a beautiful restaurant. Although she didn't start out as one of the original 'Rainbow' members, she's now become an indispensable one.

Daejeon Blues Meetings

The members of this group are related to Daejeon city, especially with its notorious prison. Attorney Han Seung Hun, former assembly member Jang Young Dal, ceo of *Sisa In* magazine Pyo Wan Su, former second deputy director at National Intelligence Service Park Jung Sam, former vice chairman of SK Jo Jung Nam belong to this group. They were all fighters for democracy and were jailed into Daejeon prison as political prisoners. Although I was never imprisoned, since I was the ICU president in Daejeon, we just named ours meetings Daejeon-Blues for fun. Sometimes we have guest members, such as former assembly member Kim Sang Hyun, actress Jang Mi Hee, and singer Jeon In Kwon.

Attorney Han has such unique life experiences. He worked through Korea's democratization process. As an attorney, he worked for those who were being oppressed by the authoritarian regime and eventually was imprisoned. The many people he defended are key figures who represent the history of Korea's modern democracy. Although he has suffered, you could not tell he had a difficult past from meeting him because of his fabulous sense of humor. He always makes us smile, and we can't imagine our Daejeon Blues meeting without him. Coincidentally, it was him who came up with the group's name. I am so honored each time I'm around him and always happy to spend time with him.

As for former assemblyman Jang, a great fighter for democratic reform, I have mentioned before how we can learn so many great life lessons by looking at his life. Even though he has served in the assembly for four terms, he is so modest and always volunteers for all kinds of small tasks within the group, like calling the members and bringing them things. He doesn't possess any air of authority or power, and he lives his life plainly with simplicity. These days, his happiness comes from the two dogs he's raising at his Yangpyeong home. When I think about how so many of us live for personal gains and short-term gratifications sometimes he seems like a true ascetic.

ceo Pyo is a graduate of SNU who studied English Literature as I did. I remember I met him after he came back from the army, and to us younger students, he seemed so mature and manly. He worked as a journalist but was dismissed by the military government and was sent to prison. These days, he is a grey-haired gentleman with a great style. He served as the ceo of various broadcasting stations until he became the ceo of *Sisa In*. He is a sensitive and gentle man whose nurturing side is his biggest charm.

Ex-Assembly Members' Meeting

This group met once a month and consisted of politicians who had all served as assembly members from the Democratic Party. The group was headed by very warm Mr. Chung Dae Chul. He always encouraged others around him and went out of his way to help them. He brought the group together, and we listened to his insights about current events during our meetings. Throughout my political career, he was the person I had closest ties with thanks to his warm nature. He comes from an extremely distinguished family and has an impressive resume and an impressive character, political experience and eloquence. It makes me a little frustrated that he hasn't had the opportunity to do something truly grand in the political field. He treated me and many colleagues to Pyeongyang style cold noodles, dumplings and Kimchi stew so often that those dishes now remind me of him. Even though I try to stay away from the political arena these days, I enjoy this group because of my fondness for him.

SNU's Enlglish Literature Major Alumni Meeting

When I first started at SNU, there were only twenty English Literature majors. Traditionally, there were not many female students in that department, but the year that I entered, six of us from my Gyunggi Girls High School matriculated. Fast-forward to now, our reunions are usually led by our male alumni friends, and I'm the only female who ever attends the meeting. Our group has eight members, and the meetings are organized by Mr. Pyo Wan Soo, the former ceo of YTN. All of us have shared memories of our youth, and our meetings are very free and informal.

Gyunggi Girls High School Alumna Meeting: Hue (休) De Mong (夢)

Some of my close friends from high school and I get together from time to time. We usually meet for a meal or coffee, celebrate each other's birthdays or other special events and play golf together. Until recently, the ladies were so busy with work we only got to meet a few times a year. But now, with more of us reaching retirement (most of us are professors or doctors) we decided to get together more often to enjoy each other's company.

Since each of us had a quite busy, forward-moving life, we named our group to mean that we will now take a real break from work and have all the fun we have dreamed of. We meet every second Thursday of the month and our meetings are quite informal since we call ourselves Hue De Mong, meaning 'rest' and 'dream.' We have been friends since high school so everyone is close, and we respect each other and everyone's accomplishment in their own professional field. When we're together, we never run out of things to talk about, and there are no pretenses. As we all are a little older, a little less competitive and a little more relaxed, we enjoy each other's company more and have more fun as we grow old together.

Mijisu (美知秀) Meeting

This group is made up of women professors in Education Technology. Most of them are teaching, but a few also work as executives at major corporations. One of my students from the 'Huh-She' group Dr. Kim Mi Jung is the youngest member of this group, and she volunteers to do a lot of work for the group as the general manager. Dr. Gwon Sung Ho from Hanyang who led the department with me and Ewha Womans University's Kim Young Soo are two other members who have also been long time friends and colleagues. Both are true pioneers in the field and are now about to retire.

Other members of the group are Dr. Yoon Yeo Soon, the director of LG Art Center, ceo of InTouch Dr. Yoon Kyung Hee, Sejong University's Dr. Lee In Sook, Ewah Women's University's Dr. Gang Myung Hee, Suncheon University's Dr. Huh Whe Ok, Chungbook University's Dr. Lee Ok Wha, Posco Human Resources Development Center's director Dr. Oh In Kyung. All of us have spent decades as leaders in the field of

Education Technology, and throughout our careers, we have shared challenges and victories together. Most importantly, all of us are beautiful ladies which is why our group is called 'Mijisu' (Mi is a Chinese letter meaning 'beauty,' ji 'intellect' and su 'outstanding').

SNU AIP Meeting

This group is made up of people I met when I was invited to give a lecture to Seoul National University's AIP (Advanced Information Program), a leadership program for ceo's. Although I first went as a lecturer, I was soon persuaded to join the program myself because these ceo-students were so wonderful. The former minister of Justice Kim Jung Gil is the head of this group, and it is a fun group of people providing mutual support to each other.

SPC (Seoul Photo Club) Meeting

SPC is a photo club that I joined because I wanted to rekindle my old hobby from college days. Through the club, I get to attend lectures given by photography professors, and it has helped me to see objects in a different light. Two people can be looking at a same thing at the same place, but when each person takes a photo of it, the results can look different because of factors like the photographer's point of view and feelings at the moment, composition in the frame, and the photographer's level of interest and concentration in the subject. Even though members of this club come from all different backgrounds, sharing the same hobby brings us together. We like to meet from time to time over meals or go on photography excursions and exchange feedback. It's nice to have a group to share this aspect of my life with.

'Kolon Sporex Aerobics' Meeting

This group was created in 2001, and as the name suggests, this group is made up of the ladies in the aerobics class at my gym. Most are around my age or a little younger, and we usually get together after our class to have lunch and chat. All the other members are housewives, and we also enjoy talking about our lives while sitting and relaxing naked in the sauna. All the ladies are experts housewives and have amazing knowledge and insights into raising children. They are wise about life, and they teach me a lot. When I wasn't working, I spent time with them almost every day, and we went to a fashion show and music concerts together. We have become close and attend each other's major life events and celebrations, and I consider them my second family.

Apart from the above mentioned meetings, there are other meetings and groups I belong to that are less regular and more spontaneous.

Becoming the Chairman of National Patriot and Veterans Culture and Arts Association

National Patriot and Veterans Culture Arts Association is a company founded in 1998. It is under the jurisdiction of Ministry of Culture and Sports and was created to bring renowned artists, their families and others from the art scene together to collaborate and contribute to the Korean cultural arts. The company works on overseas marketing and distribution of Korean art. It also holds exhibitions and contests for artists, runs welfare projects for artists' families and gives awards.

Jang Young Dal was its chairman, and I was the co-chair. After he resigned from the role, I was asked to fill his shoes, and in September 2009, I became the chair. This is an honorary role and the company's secretary general is responsible for handling its actual affairs.

This company, which was originally created through funding from the

Ministry of Patriots and Veterans Affairs, has several thousand members, and most of them are artists specializing in western painting, Asian painting or calligraphy.

Fabulous Times Spent with Artists

When I was in middle and high school, I was quite good at art. In college, I also learned western style painting as well. But my artistic skills seemed to be limited to imitation, and I didn't ever become truly creative with my art. Because of this, I still admire people with creative profession. Maybe that's why I accepted the chairman position because I felt privileged to be working with so many talented artists.

I had a lot of great experiences through this association. I visited Japan, China and the Middle East to hold exhibitions and also participated in discussions and critiques about art. I found these experiences to be very educational and interesting.

One time, a mature female artist gave me a jade ring and a bracelet just because she liked me. I was so touched but surprised as well to receive such a precious gift. Looking back, maybe her giving me this precious gift without wanting anything in return reflected the temperament of an artistic person.

The organization also held many exhibitions in Korea. It held numerous exhibitions in small and big galleries in Insa-dong and at the Seoul Arts Center. Some of the artists kindly gave me their work as gifts, and I did my best to serve these artists whom I admired so much. Working for them was so enjoyable that the two years I spent there passed by too quickly.

When I was without a job, I played a lot of golf, and there were a few different groups of people I played with. We would coordinate our schedule and form groups spontaneously to go on the field. During this time of break, I still remained very busy. I met with many different groups, learned to dance, and chaired an organization.

As I was going about my days as an unemployed free person, many people asked me if I was ever going to go back to university life, but I didn't make any effort to be employed during this time. Many people also asked me if I was going to go back to Hanyang, but since my own students had grown and become professors themselves, it seemed strange for me to return. I also felt I had been there and done my time and no longer had the desire to go back. I wanted to cherish this moment when I didn't have any particular goals or obligations and could simply indulge in life's small daily pleasures.

Lamenting Resident Roh's Death

In the movie *Four Weddings and a Funeral*, there is a scene where they recite poet W.H. Auden's *Funeral Blues*.

Stop all the clocks, cut off the telephone
Prevent the dog from barking with a juicy bone
Silence the pianos and with muffled drum
Bring out the coffin, let the mourners come.

Let aeroplanes circle moaning overhead
Scribbling on the sky the message 'He is Dead.'
Put crepe bows around the white necks of the public doves
Let the traffic policemen wear black cotton gloves

He was my North, my South, my East and West
My working week and my Sunday rest,
My noon, my midnight, my talk, my song;
I thought that love would last forever: I was wrong
The stars are not wanted now; put out everyone
Pack up the moon and dismantle the sun,
Pour away the ocean and sweep up the wood;
For nothing now can ever come to any good.

On May 23, 2009, something so tragic and shocking happened in Bongha Village in Gyungnam that couldn't be described fully even by this poem. Presidet Roh had passed away. After finishing his term, he moved back to his hometown in the countryside and resumed his life working on a farm and occasionally sharing Makguli (Korean traditional liquor) with his friends and supporters. Then somehow, he found himself caught up in an official investigation concerning a family member, and it led him to take his own life. In Confucius's teaching, when the father passes away, the family experiences it as a tragedy akin to having the entire sky fall upon them. When I heard about his death, I felt a similar shock and sadness. The next day, one of my former assistants from my campaign days drove me three hours to Bongha village. I left a single chrysanthemum flower by the now deceased president, and without saying hello or talking to anyone, drove back to Seoul in full sorrow. The next few days were spent in a daze, but I pulled it together to make it to his funeral held in front of the city hall, packed with mourning people. I also wrote a contribution in time for his funeral and submitted it to *The Digital Times* paper. Following is an excerpt from my contribution.

> Now our ex-President Roh has left us. Not millions of citizens' tears and sympathy can bring him back to us. It is too late to save him, but what gives me some comfort is we can take this moment to remember him for who he really was.
>
> What kind of a leader do we truly miss? We miss a leader like Roh who stuck by his principles and stood strong and firm in the midst of criticism and accusations. President Roh suffered in his heart.
>
> Dear president, I'm sorry you were alone during your last moments here. I'm sorry we weren't there for you. Your dreams, loneliness and suffering, I miss them all. I hope you rest in peace. Leave it to the rest of us to carry on and finish the work you couldn't in your lifetime.
>
> Today, there are different opinions about him, but in time, history will see him for a new kind of president he was, one who rejected authoritarian governance and was a man of grit and principles.

Inauguration at National Patriot and Veterans Culture Arts Association.

1

2

1 With participating artists at the Korean Modern Art exhibition held in Dubai.
2 At the Korean-Chinese Women Artists exhibition held in Yu'an, China.
3 An interview at the Korean Modern Art exhibition in Dubai.
4 At the Korean Modern Art Exhibition in Abu Dubai.

3

4

1

2

1 With some of 'Huh Sa Mo' members.
2 At my birthday party with some of 'Huh-Dang' members.

One of the photos I took during an SPC shooting event.

Act 8

Making New Contributions to Songdo International City

Whose woods these are I think I know.

His house is in the village though.

He will not see me stopping here

to watch his woods fill up with snow.

…

The woods are lovely, dark and deep.

But I have promises to keep,

and miles to go before I sleep.

And miles to go before I sleep.

— Robert Frost, *Stopping by Woods on a Snowy Evening*

Educating Young Leaders
at Chadwick International School

A Letter from California

"I wonder if there is anything new I can do."

I had been living the life of a retiree for a while now, living the later third of my life and filling it with ambitionless fun. Then suddenly, I got an ache: an idea came to me that I would like to use all my life experiences, skills and networks to make some sort of contribution. It was a sudden urge to live a life of service. Then one day, I received a letter from a long time friend Dick Warmington from the States.

Dick was a California boy who studied at Stanford University and received an MBA from Harvard. Afterwards, he worked for HP for thirty-three years. During his career, he lived and worked in Korea for four years from 1988 to 1992 as the ceo of Samsung-HP Korea, a joint business created by the two giant corporations.

While they were in Korea, Dick and his wife Carolyn adopted two Korean children, a six year-old girl and a newborn infant boy. I watched them go through the adoption process and raise their children with all their love and care. They are such angelic loving parents.

1

2

채드윅 국제학교 방문
2011. 3. 10

3

1 At our home, with Dick, his daughter and my daughter (1988).
2 With Dick's wife Carolyn and her son Michael (1988).
3 With Dick, my old friend and the first head of Chadwick School (2012).

After working in Korea, Dick and his family moved to Hong Kong where he worked as the ceo of HP's Asia Pacific headquarter. Afterwards, he returned to California and stayed there until he retired in 2000. After his retirement, Dick volunteered as an independent school trustee.

I had met Dick when I was working at Hanyang and we developed a friendship based on our shared professional field. Later, he also helped me arrange visits to HP's headquarter and bench-market their educational center. We had many discussions back in those days about corporate education. The letter I received from Dick that day read like this.

> Hi Unna, How are you? I hope you're doing well.
>
> It's been over ten years since I returned from Hong Kong and settled back down in my hometown in Silicone Valley. After my retirement, I joined the board of directors at my son's school and served as the chair for several years. I've also been on the board at another school.
>
> A little while ago, Chadwick School in L.A. contacted me. They have been looking at opening a branch school in Songdo for a while now and told me that they have finally decided to go forward with it. They gave me a call because I attended Chadwick as a student, and I also worked and lived in Korea for four years. They asked if I would be interested in moving back to Korea for a few years to help them get the school started.
>
> It was a difficult offer to refuse since I've always been interested in managing a private school, and I have a lot of love for Korea, having lived there and adopted my children from there. It made sense that I would be the right person to go there and take that job. On top of that, our son Michael has recently left for college, so Carolyn and I have been feeling a little lonely. Anyway, we decided to accept the offer and I'll be coming to Chadwick as the chairman of the school's preparation committee. Once the school opens, I will be the head.
>
> As soon as we decided to take the offer, Carolyn and I both immediately thought of you. I would love for you to join us and help the school take off. So let's get together soon to talk more about this.
>
> from Dick

This unexpected letter came at the perfect time since I was looking for something new to do. I replied to him right away.

Hi Dick, thanks for your letter.

As you know, I'm originally an educator. Recently, I've been taking a break from work since I resigned from my university president position almost two years ago for political reasons. But I'm thrilled to help you with your new job and help establish this school. I will think of it as my new part time work.

Before I get involved, I need to know what kind of an institution Chadwick is. Let me look into it first, and I'll figure out how I can best help you.

from Unna

This exchange took place in early January 2010. At this time, the school building had already been built. Gale International, which was working with Posco on Songdo's development had invested 170 million dollars to buy the land and build the school. The school was going to have cutting-edge, top of the line facilities, including a large theater, a library, a gym, a swimming pool, a tennis court, a track field and multiple stadiums.

The only problem was the school didn't have an operator or a license. All the hardware was there, but it was missing the software. It was under these circumstances that Gale International contacted the prestigious Chadwick School in Los Angeles to see if they wanted to open a branch school in Songdo. Chadwick agreed, and finally, the basic infrastructure for the school was set in place.

Deciding to Help Open the Chadwick International School

Dick arrived in Korea as the chairman to oversee the preparations. Together, we took a look around the school campus which had yet to put up its sign. Afterwards, we flew to the States to take a tour of Chadwick's mother campus.

The school was located in Palos Verdes on the top of a hill overlooking the city of L.A.. I talked with people at the school and observed their classes. I learned that at this school, the classes were a lot more student-centric. Their classes stressed proactive learning and learning through inquiry and experience. In Korea, these styles of learning had been introduced at some schools, but often, they remained only slogans and concepts and not implemented in reality. Sadly, no matter what brilliant new educational methods got introduced, the Korean educational culture remained too focused on scores and rankings to adapt these new ways. After looking around Chadwick, I decided I would help this fine school launch its branch in Korea. I thought this would be a fitting final contribution to make as an educator to Korean education.

Moving Through Ups and Downs to Lay the School's Foundations

Before I talk the about Chadwick School, I will explain briefly about Incheon Free Economic Zone. This was the first Free Economic Zone created in Korea, and was comprised of three areas: Songdo, Youngjong and Chungla. The government planned to develop these three areas by 2020 as commerce and business cities connected to the Incheon airport by the beautiful Incheon bridge which excites me each time I cross it.

Songdo International City boasts a beautiful curved shaped convention center, themed after the waves of the Yellow Sea. It also has Chadwick School Songdo, Asia's first Jack Nicklaus' JN Golf Club, a 68-storey landmark building NEATT, beautiful residential and commercial complexes with Gaudi-like architecture, a waterway and water taxi reminiscent of New York's Central Park, and its own Central Park with bike paths. It is referred to as the world's biggest development project, carried out mostly by private developers.

With Chairman Stan Gale.

All the buildings in the business quarter, including Chadwick, are LEED certified and follow a strict environmental code. CISCO, a global IT corporation, has also brought in their cutting-edge technology to help Songdo become the 'Smart & Connected' city it claims to be.

The first time I visited the school building, I thought it was beautiful and built to satisfy all the educational purposes it would serve. Later, I found out that experts from Harvard contributed in the early stages of the school's designing process. A good example of this carful design is having a toilet inside each primary school classroom.

Stan Gale, the chairman of Gale International, was responsible for the overall construction and design of the business district. He built the school first then went back to L.A. to look for a suitable manager for the school. After he saw the school in L.A., he decided to bring Chadwick on board.

Even though there was an agreement between the school and the contractor, Chadwick still needed to get an official approval from the Ministry of Education to open its door. This was going to be a difficult road, and it ended brining me and Mr. Gale close together. Gale International had received a project financing loan from Korea's Shinhan Bank and used it to build international business districts. Before inviting Chadwick to run the school, the company requested and received another 40 million dollars to invest in running the school for the next five years. With this funding, the company could more easily recruit Chadwick and establish an agreement to work together.

However, the process of actually obtaining the 40 million was a difficult one. It was during the time of world financial crisis in 2007, and banks were unwilling to loan money. In addition to Shinhan Bank, there were around fifteen other creditor banks from which Gale International was getting its funding, and all of them were afraid the buildings would not be rented out, and they wouldn't get their money back.

The Ministry of Education then said it wouldn't grant the school an operating license unless the company acquired all the necessary funding. Gale International suddenly found itself caught up in a quagmire without a way out. As I realized they needed my help desperately, I mobilized my personal network and finally got one of the highest officials at Shinhan to approve the extra loan. Once this happened, the other fourteen banks soon followed.

Finally Getting the Approval

The process of getting the license for the school was also a long one with a lot of push and pull that went on with the ministry's bureaucracy. Initially, Chadwick chose to work with the ministry by hiring a famous Korean law firm. This only delayed the progress because the officials at the ministry didn't like being contacted by a law firm as a school representative. I had to step in to expedite and mediate, and thankfully, my long-time connection to the educational field was helpful in making this work.

The school was set to open in September of 2010, and there was a lot of work to do before the opening. We calculated that we needed the government's permission by April so we could begin recruiting students. The students then needed to go through the admission process. There was not much time, but the Ministry of Education (MOE) was taking their time and didn't seem to be in any rush. Any international school built within an economic free zone would be subjected to special laws, and it was the Ministry of Knowledge Economy (MKE) that was in charge of these laws. Although MKE was supportive of starting the school, which was necessary for bringing in foreign investors to the area, MOE had a much different attitude.

I got busy meeting with officials at the Ministry of Education and convincing them to accelerate the permission process. Finally, they approved the opening with 2080 students as the cap. Another one of their requirements was that the school could only accept 30% of Korean students.

We now had the funding and the much-needed approval from the Ministry of Education, and things seemed to be moving along smoothly. Then all of sudden, we were hit with an unforeseen obstacle. The ministry suddenly decided that Chadwick School Songdo couldn't pay an annual loyalty to its mother school in L.A. . I immediately asked how they could prohibit their paying a management fee, which was something that was internationally approved, but the only response I got was ministry's policy doesn't allow any money to be transfered from one school to another. Finally, Gale International came up with the idea that they would pay the fee to L.A. instead of having Songdo Chadwick pay them directly, and the problem was solved.

Becoming a Full-Time Advisor to Chadwick International School

After facing many hurdles, we received the final permission to establish the school in June. As Dick requested, I took on my new job as the chief advisor to the school, a full time job to take care of all the external affairs, including government relationships.

Things really needed to start moving fast now. We hired all the teachers very quickly, and we moved on to selecting all the students, and the school opened its door in September.

After the school opened, we quickly noticed that the '30% Korean students rule' was problematic. Because there weren't enough foreigners living in Songdo yet, we needed to pick more Korean students to fill the gap, but the law prohibited us from having more than 30%. We decided to work on changing the law and were eventually able to convince the government (both MKE & MOE) to increase this number to 50% for the time being. In doing this, my experience at the National Assembly as a law maker played an essential role. The Korean government threw in a catch, however. The decision to allow extra 20% would have to come from the superintendent of education of our district. Right away, we initiated another round of negotiations with Incheon's superintendent to obtain his approval and finally got it.

An Interview with the Brazilian National Broadcasting Network about Korean Education.

Chadwick's Student-Centered Learning

Chadwick School has four educational goals for its students: fostering academic excellence, developing leadership character, helping self-discovery through experience and developing a global mind.

Chadwick highly values self-initiated learning. Students don't rely on one textbook. Instead, they learn to reference many different resources and books. Each student gets a personal computer, and each elementary school student is provided with an Ipad since it is easy for children to use. The focus of learning is on exploration, and classes are interdisciplinary in nature so students learn to draw broader connections between the subjects they learn. For instance, if the topic of the lecture is 'democracy,' it is covered in the Social Science class and also in their Gym and Art classes. Students also have a greater say in how their classes are carried out. For instance, in the Gym class, students offer their opinions about what the activity of the day should be. Then, they discuss the different ideas and form a consensus as to what they will do that day. Through this simple exercise, they get to learn how democracy operates. In their art class, they could be asked to think about a question, like whether a totalitarian country could also have art. They would discuss how art is used for marketing and propaganda in these societies and do research on posters or artists from there. They would perhaps do some exercises where they have to create propaganda posters based on their imagination. Through these projects, students learn to make connections between a historical event, artistic works and relationships between countries.

Students as Owners of Their Own Learning

Chadwick believes that students are owners of their own education. Students come up with their own questions and try to find their own answers. This style of learning requires the students to do a lot of research.

Chadwick students conduct their own research and present their results. This is the opposite way of learning from the typical Korean ways, and it fosters critical thinking abilities. At Chadwick, students in grade five and up make small groups and they get to invite other students, teachers and parents to hear their presentation on their research findings.

For example, one team could pick water preservation as their topic of research. They would then visit the local wastewater treatment facilities and interview public officials who work there for their research. After doing this, they come up with their own conclusions to the original question, and sometimes even craft their own original solutions. Finally, they give their presentations based on their research experience. These projects really help them develop their creativity and thinking.

Emphasizing Core Values

Chadwick also emphasizes five core values that are the foundations of strong leadership. They are honesty, respect, responsibility, compassion and fairness. When students get in trouble, they have to participate in deciding the consequences for their own actions. The student in trouble is asked to think about how their actions have violated one of the five core values. The responsibility to act according to these core values applies to teachers as well.

At Chadwick, creative and artistic endeavors are highly valued, and its music, art, physical education and performance arts are all taken seriously. For example, a student in a play would participate in the whole production process, from producing a play to preparing the costumes. They learn to work with others in a team and learn to trust their decisions, which builds their confidence, collaboration and leadership skills.

Another area the school emphasizes is community service and volunteering. Students get many opportunities for volunteer work as the need arises around them. For instance, there are a lot of migratory birds and nests around the school, and if they see garbage is accumulating near them, students can form groups to clean the area. Other things they do include helping out poor senior citizens who live alone, tutoring English to under-privileged children, and helping North Korean refugees. Students get to choose how they'd like to volunteer according to their interest.

Outdoor activities are also important. Each spring and fall, students participate in a week-long trip to a new destination and experience new surroundings. High school begins in the 9th grade for Chadwick students. In fall of 2013, 9th graders went to the Southern Sea in Gyeongsang-nam-do province. They went kayaking, fishing, hiking, and worked on a farm and visited a Buddhist temple. Some students painted a mural for the village. Students also practiced their critical thinking skills in their new environment by asking questions like, "Why does this village only have older people?," "Why do these farmers work so hard but still are poor?"

In the spring of 2013, the 9th grade class went to Jiri Mountain, and they were in charge of everything involved in camping, from preparing the meals to keeping the environment clean and volunteering in the area. These experiences helped them to become more self-sufficient and appreciative of nature. Chadwick teaches its students to utilize both their mind and their body.

"Never Stop Asking Questions to Yourself"

Chadwick School Songdo and its mother school in the States share a lot of similarities in the way they operate. Songdo teachers have discussions about their class curriculum with the teachers in L.A. through CISCO's modern technology called 'Tele-Presence' system. The middle and high school students in Songdo also work on at least one academic project per year in collaboration with L.A. students. Overall, there is a lot of inter-action between the teachers and students from the two schools.

To help students discover their core values, the school encourages them to ask introspective questions. Students are encouraged to reflect on questions like "Who am I?," "What is the relationship between me and my surroundings?," "What am I good at and what do I like to do?" These questions help student figure out for themselves what they want to do in the future. Unlike the typical Korean mindset, Chadwick students appreciate that the best university for them is the one that best suits their individual needs, and not just Harvard or Yale. Chadwick will have its first graduating class in the spring of 2016.

Korea Needs This Kind of Advanced Education

When a student's parent visits Chadwick, the meeting is usually between the teacher, the student and the parent. At the meeting, the teacher asks the student to talk about his/her own recent academic activities rather than the teacher speaking on the student's behalf. This is called 'student-led presentation' and helps the parent hear directly from the child all the proactive learning that has happened. This kind of meeting also helps the parent understand the kind of education that takes place at Chadwick, which might be unfamiliar to the parent at first. This is, no doubt, completely different from the conventional style of parent-teacher meeting that takes place where the student is usually excluded from the discussion. I would like to see Chadwick style education and meeting be incorporated in Korean schools.

I like to invite different opinion leaders to Chadwick. I usually invite university presidents, professors, education superintendents, principals and teachers as well as company ceo's and chairmans so they can see what education looks like at Chadwick. I also invite school commissioners and hold seminars. This year, meetings for all the English teachers in the Incheon area were held at Chadwick.

Chadwick is a very expensive school, and the cost of tuition is very high.

One of the reasons for this expensive tuition is that most of the teachers are recruited from abroad, and the school pays for their housing. The royalty paid to Chadwick's L.A. campus and imported teaching materials from the U.S. also contribute to the expense. If all the teachers were locals, it would significantly reduce the cost of operation and drive the tuition down. If this was possible, we can envision having Chadwick-style schools in Korea for Korean students. In other words, we could have the most innovative schools where tuition is much less expensive. I hope this will come true for Korea in the near future. This is why I am here at Chadwick.

Making My Contribution to
Songdo's Development

Songdo as an Ideal Future City

The American TV station ABC did a report on Songo International City calling it an ideal example of what future cities should look like. It pointed out that its business zone development project was the world's largest private real estate project. ABC also explained that Songdo could end up looking very similar to the futuristic cities we've seen in movies like *The 5th Element and Minority Report*, and that its biggest advantage was it was being built with a view towards the rest of the world.

The 'Economist' also called Songdo the second most promising city in the world in terms of its potential for growth. The city was voted in a national survey as the most favorable city to conduct business in.

Many world organizations have also moved into the city. There are several UN-affiliated organizations and ten other world organizations in Songdo now. In December 2013, GCF (Green Climate Fund) and World Bank also moved in. The mayor of Incheon, Mr. Song Young Gil, who also served with me in the National Assembly, has an exciting vision for the city and successfully brought these organizations to Songdo. Once

A-WEB(Association of World Election Body)'s Secretariat moves in, Songdo can finally call itself an international city.

Educationally, there are world-class universities and schools being built in Songdo. Chadwick is one, and Yonsei University's international campus and the State University of New York have opened, and in 2014, other American universities like George Mason University, Utah University and Belgium's Ghent University will open as well.

Songdo is also developing its own Bio Complex. Adding to its already existing Celltrion base, the city has also brought in Samsung Bio Logics and Donga Pharmaceutical and is emerging as Korea's next Bio Mecca. Similar activities have taken place in its semi-conductor arena, where Songdo has attracted Japan's TOK, America's Amkor, and other foreign companies in order to establish itself as a major high-tech city.

The world's best semi-conductor corporation, Emcor, has already built five buildings in Songdo, including its global R&D center. Japanese company TOK has also built its R&D and production facilities for its semi-conductors.

Songdo also has Korea's highest building, the North-East Asia Trade (NEAT) Tower. This 68-storey building is expected to finish construction by July 2014 and will house a five-star hotel Oakwood as well as CISCO, 3M and other multinational corporations. Daewoo International is another company that will move into this landmark building with its 1000 employees.

A nearby building and an R&D center called Songdo Techno Park IT Center will house Kolon Global, Kolon Water and Energy with their 1000-plus employees. And lastly, another landmark Posco E.C Tower is a 39-storey twin tower that houses Posco and their affiliate businesses.

Songdo is indeed growing and becoming a cutting-edge city with an outlook towards the future, and I have been working with mayor Song to continue attracting foreign capital and act as his advisor.

1

2

1　Night view of Incheon's Free Economic Zone.
2　With the mayor of Incheon Song Young Gil and chairman of CISCO John
　　chambers after signing the agreement.

Mayor Song, a Reliable Advocate for
All of Incheon Residents

Songdo city's construction began with a vision to become a 'smart and connected city.' I was happy I was able to play a part in bringing the city closer to its vision. My work as an aid to my long time friend Mr. Song was therefore very meaningful to me. When I was working at the assembly, Mr. Song attended every single one of the IPAIT events I hosted, and I was really appreciative. It showed his dedication especially since all the events were done in English. A lot of other assembly members only showed up at the tape cutting ceremony to shake hands, take a few photos and left early. Mr. Song was different. He participated actively in discussions with other foreign congressmen. After watching me host these international forums, he told me one day it motivated him to study more English. He employed a native-speaking English tutor and started studying. Then later, I got to see just how much he'd improved when I went to a meeting in the States between Incheon and CISCO's headquarter. The meeting was about an agreement to build greener IT infrastructure. At the meeting, Mr. Song led the entire event by himself in English, and I was amazed at his accomplishment. I think he impressed all the Korean reporters there that day with his English fluency.

Out of all the politicians I know, Mr. Song is the most passionate about self-improvement. Not only is he great at English, but he also speaks Chinese very well. He studied management at Yonsei. However, he is truly a life-long learner, and he enrolled at another school to learn Chinese while he was a congressman. He also studied Japanese and has recently taken up Russian. One time, he explained to me that he's preparing for the day North and South Korea finally reunite, which is why he's learning the languages of the countries surrounding North and South Korea. He's also proficient in French and has received the la Legion d'Honneur (the Legione of Honor) award, France's most prestigious award. On the day he received this award, he gave a full speech in French. When we visited the Middle East to speak with our investors, I also saw him talk with the locals in

Arabic. He really is passionate about everything he does and gives it his best.

I truly believe that residents of Incheon are blessed to have Mr. Song as their mayor. He is mindful of Incheon's geographically central location within the Korean peninsula and its proximity to North Korea. He is also economically keen and has a strategic outlook regarding North-South relations with an eye to possible economic gains. He is very forward-looking, and in trying to pave the way for reunification, he is considering inviting the North Korean players to the Incheon Asian Games to facilitate the dialogue between the two countries. Even during his days at the National Assembly, he rose past party interests and voted in favor of FTA, showing his far-sighted perspective.

Mr. Song likes to make fun of himself by calling himself a country boy, and he surely identifies himself as part of the working class. He genuinely wants to look after those who are struggling and living without privileges. He is such a hard worker who doesn't have any ulterior motives. A quote by poet John Keats, "Beauty is truth, Truth Beauty" seems to describe him and his way of being. Even though he is ten years my junior, his purity and sincerity, his passion and vision for his country, his compassion for Korea's struggling working class have all inspired great trust and admiration in me. I am deeply happy to lend my help to such an extraordinary young leader, and believe Incheon residents have a precious gem in their mayor.

I am glad I made the decision to work for Songdo and Chadwick after getting Dick's letter, and I hope that my life from here on will also be lived in a spirit of service.

=== Scene 23 ===

Life Is about Learning and Loving

Starting and Chairing Start-Up Forum

'Jobless youth,' 'more jobs for the young.' These are the major challenges facing the Korean society today. As an IT specialist and a person who's spent my whole life educating our youth, this issue weighs heavily on my mind. And I think one solution to the problem is fostering the growth of Start-up companies.

On March 15, 2012, there was an important meeting held at the Grand Intercontinental Hotel in Seoul. The director Kim Bok Man at *The Electronic Times* had been spearheading the efforts to help Korean Start-ups for years with great passion. As I have also been very interested in this area since Kim Dae Jung's administration, we decided to come together and start a forum. The meeting marked the beginning of Start-up Forum, a corporation we built to lend more fuel to the growth of Start-ups and build an ecosystem where fledgling companies can seek the resources they need along the way.

Start-up Forum's main objective is to provide a space where anyone who wishes to launch their own Start-up can easily meet with a mentor

1

2

1 The launching celebration for Start-up Forum.
2 With the Forum's starting members.
3 Interviewing the ceo of XL Games, Song Jae Gyung.
4 Interviewing the mayor of Incheon, Song Young Gil.
5 Interviewing the ceo of Skylake Incubest, Jin Dae Jae.

3

4

5

and get practical advice. It also allows new entrepreneurs to receive guidance from other knowledgeable and helpful individuals who are working for government organizations and university research centers along the way. The Small and Medium Business Administration and a number of banks will also participate and provide funds for the companies. Prior to Start-up Forum, there were similar efforts in Korea to support new businesses, but they were always fruitless. It took us about a year of preparation to launch this company, and once it opened, I became the chairman. The following July, Start-up Forum officially became a corporation under Ministry of Trade, Industry and Energy (MOTIE).

Selecting the Top Ten Start-Ups to Support

At Start-up Forum's End of the Year Party in December 2013, we awarded ten most promising Start-ups. These companies were chosen out of 250 applicants by a panel of judges who came from different fields. The top five companies would receive 100 thousand dollars in funding. All the judges agreed there were a lot of high quality applicants and wished there was room for more than ten companies. The chances are very good that these companies will go on to generate millions in revenue and eventually go IPO or receive an M&A offer to go international within a few years.

These days, the number one global issue seems to be job creation and growing the creative economy. I think our Start-up companies can take the leading position in this. The party was made even more special since we got to appoint a very famous Hallyu (Korean Wave) star singer Kim Jung Hoon as our honorary ambassador. It's exciting for me to think that through Start-up Forum, I can help young Korean entrepreneurs' dreams come true and help create more jobs in our country.

Mark Zuckerberg started Facebook as a Start-up when he was at Harvard, and he was only able to grow it into what it is today because he had an investor to back him up. I will do my best to create a support base in Korea for our promising entrepreneurs so they can spread their wings like Zuckerberg did.

Dreaming of a Life of Service

Because I had spent almost thirty years as a university professor, my friends and acquaintances often ask me why I'm not going back to university to teach. To me, this is a very Korean (minded) question. I plan on making my last contribution to Korean education at Chadwick and not at a university. It's been a long time since I've renounced the conventional materialistic notion of 'success,' as most Korean people conceive. In heroic novels like the *Chinese History of Three States* (三國志), many heroes died without achieving such notion of success. Some people think that I shouldn't stay only in Songdo or at a school, that I should 'go on to do more important things.' Some people have even told me that it would be a 'national loss' if I stayed where I currently am. I reply that I have been at the top, and now I wish to leave that room for other younger people to take on and do their job. I think it can be dangerous to hold on to the idea that I must do everything. I'm happier doing what I'm doing right now. I'm happy to be making contributions in my own way exactly where I am.

I heard someone preach once that life equals learning and loving. Looking back at my own life, I agree that life is a never-ending process of learning, loving your work and others with passion, and being of service to others. My journey of learning and loving will probably continue until the day I die. As a free person and as a beautiful person.

1 Chadwick's school yard.
2 Chadwick's indoor pool.
3 Talking with Chadwick students.

Huh Unna That I Know

Jang Young Dal

Former Assembly Member

Dr. Huh has been a leader in multiple fields, working as a professor, assembly member, chairwoman of an international organization and a director of sports organization. Out of all of these titles, I like the title president of ICU the best. ICU has now been incorporated into KAIST, but when she was the president, ICU really helped build the basis for the Korean IT industry. The IPAIT, which was also created by Dr. Huh, made similar contribution. Our Daejeon Blues group, which started when she was working at ICU, has meetings where our members talk about life, and Dr. Huh is a bright and pure intellectual in our group like a ray of sunlight.

Oh In Kyung

Director at Posco Research Institute

Dr. Huh exemplifies beauty and giving.

About twenty years ago, I encountered the department of Educational Technology at Hanyang University for the first time. It was a love at first sight for me when I saw Dr. Huh in her slim blue jeans and an Indian-style suede jacket as she came to greet me. There were only a few women PhD's in our department then. She invited us to her home, got us into schools, found us jobs and gave us beautiful gifts. While she was busy holding many important positions abroad and in Korea, she maintained her beautiful grace and her kind generosity.

Dr. Huh broke out of the traditional female role and created a new kind of role model for women, and I sincerely admire her for this. Even though all of us are now over 50 years old, the members of MiJiSu still receive her gifts year after year. Dr. Huh, you're a true mentor, and I love you.

Yoon Yeo Soon

Former President of LG Art Center

Professor Huh! Assembly Woman Huh! President Huh!

Whatever title she has, she does her job right. I see the secret behind her amazing accomplishments as her limitless passion, love of challenges, incredible drive, discerning eye for what's coming in the future, and her extraordinary leadership. But most importantly, what I've noticed and have been greatly impressed by is the innocent and pure passion she has for what she does that is not tainted by selfish agenda. This is why I consider her more than just a senior colleague, but a friend I relate to and look up to.

Gwon Sung Ho

Professor at Hanyang University

I believe the true meaning of this book is to encourage people to live freely, courageously and positively and to inspire people to pave their own unique path that's different from everyone else's. It is truly inspiring the way Dr. Huh has paved a new way and opened new doors for others throughout her career and life. President Huh's endless passion and vision mean there's far more for us to look forward to beyond the 8 acts and 23 scenes.

Lee Ji Eun
Professor at Hanyang Cyber University

The first time I saw Dr. Huh on TV, I was a senior in high school. When I saw her on the screen, I thought, 'This must be fate.' I was mesmerized by her at the first sight and eventually became her student and spent four years at the institute, then another four years as her assistant at the assembly. During my time working with her, she taught me to love myself and live with more passion.

She has been a 'great rock face' in my life, and now I'm following in her footsteps and teaching my own students at a university. I am only here today because of Dr. Huh. Professor, I love you.

Pyo Wan Su
CEO of *Sisa In*

President Huh is one of the few women whom I call by her first name. Even though we are pretty close, I always thought of her as an elegant swan. I had no idea that she had been pedaling so hard under the water. Parts of this book were surprisingly poignant, but overall, it's a beautiful story of Unna's life.

Jang Eun Jung
Professor at Dongduk Women's University

Unna that I know has been my life's anchor and the best guide in life. At each turning point in my life, she was there to counsel me about what direction and order I should follow next. I have always wanted to emulate her even in the smallest ways, and being so inspired by her helped me to be my best at each moment. She taught me how to respond to life's ups and downs, and I'm still trying to emulate her. She showed me how I can share my happiness with others and that there's joy in sharing. I can't ever remember her being upset, and she's always there to empathize when I'm down in life. Wherever she is, she is outgoing and brings life to the occasion.

When she was a professor, she had such faith in her students she assigned unbelievable amounts of work to them, and as her student, I was able to accomplish a lot with her help. When I started working, she taught me how to overcome the handicaps of being a woman at a workplace, how to prove myself through my work. Every time I face an obstacle in life, I think about what Dr. Huh would do, and it fills me with positive energy to power through.

I think her play is still in progress, and I can't wait to read what lies beyond the 8th act. I am a true believer in Dr. Huh, and I will always to try to emulate her for the rest of my life in creating my own life's play.

Gang Myeong Hee
Professor at Ewha Womans University

Dr. Huh was my senior colleague in Educational Technology, and she has always exuded a fresh and provocative aura. She always has the curiosity of a little girl and enjoys meeting and working with new people. When she finds a new interest, she goes into action, and with her unparalleled drive, always manages to deliver great results in whatever she's doing. I love and admire the fact that she prefers an unpaved road over an easy one and enjoys being a pioneer.

Yoo Pyeong Joon
Professor at Sookmyung Women's University

Every time I think of Dr. Huh, it reminds me of Robert Frost's *Road Not Taken*. She reminds me of this poem because of all the lives she's touched being the kind of teacher she was. Every time I need to shake up my life with a new change or I make an important decision about my future, I ask myself, "What would Dr. Huh do?" She is logical, enterprising, and she is a creator. She inspires people to come up with ideas they had never thought of before. Joyous, flexible, soft, lovely and warm are the words that come to my head when I think of her. I doubt there is any other teacher who is so sincerely loved and always admired by their students.

Kim Mi Jung
Director of CREDU HR Research Center

Dr. Huh has been my boss and my academic advisor. But over the last thirty years, she has not taught me a single thing. She has simply shown me everything I needed to know through living her own life-everything from the way she makes decisions to working with other people. During my university years, I was enraptured by her unique ways, and she gave me a vision of what I wanted to become in the future. When I began working at the institute as a graduate student, she helped me develop problem-solving skills so I could pick out problems and find solutions on my own. When I was studying in the U.S., she came to visit me, and when she left, she handed me a small card which brought me to tears (she probably doesn't remember). More recently, she helped me understand HRD much better at work. Now that I'm approaching my fifties, she inspires me to imagine more hopeful and brighter last decades of my life. I am very lucky to have such an inspirational person close to me.

Kim Young Soo
Professor at Ewha Womans University

Dr. Huh Unna. She is the renaissance woman. This isn't just my personal opinion. She matches the definition of a renaissance woman found in urban dictionary.com and thefreedictionary.com.

She possesses great intellect and a million talents and has demonstrated them through different positions-as a professor, assembly woman, university president, and a CTO of an international school. She's also artistic and has been the chair of an art organization and an amateur photographer. She is dedicated to volunteering for the community, has great taste in fashion and an enviable figure. She is truly a renaissance woman with beauty, brains and heart.

Dr. Huh, you and I have come a long way for the past thirty years in the Educational Technology field. I hope we remain friends for the next thirty as well.

Yoon Gyung Hee
CEO of InTouch

Teacher, Professor, Assembly Member, President, Upper Colleague!

There are many titles I call President Huh since I've known her for a long time. Our first meeting was in the 80's at the Korea Education Development Institute. I was a not so sharp graduate student, and she was a sophisticated and smart head of International Cooperation. Our friendship has lasted over thirty years.

President Huh I know has always been passionate and stood out with her young mind. She's never hesitated to face a challenge or take action, and she is this era's true treasure who's made incredible contributions in so many different fields. She has great artistic and literary sensibilities, and as a person, she embodies a sense of freedom and warmth which makes her so appealing.

Even when she was tangled in misunderstandings and slanders, she remained cool and silent, focused only on her vision and the path she was on. And when she decided it was time to leave because her job was done, she didn't hesitate to move on. She never hesitated to help a junior colleague or a student in need. Personally, she has taught me a lot about being a consultant and looking at the world through a different perspective. Looking back, I want to confess to her that she's been a truly precious teacher and a role model to me. Dear teacher, I love and admire you.

Bae Hee Sook
CEO of E-NARU.com

When you run a business, you sometimes get burnt by people. Then later, you are helped back up by people. This reminds me that people play such an important and powerful role in our lives. President Huh is one of those people who's shown me how influential and beautiful a person can be in another person's life.

Through example, she's shown me that we need to always try to walk the path of what is just and right, even in the face of horrible setbacks in life. She's also shown me how beautiful life can be when you do make these right decisions. I want to deeply praise President Huh for always embodying the true meaning of virtue and being a beautiful person.

Lim Soo Gyung

Executive Director at KT

I still remember clearly the first time I saw President Huh. She was delivering a message that was so articulate and eloquent. The ivory colored two-piece suit she wore that day looked immaculate on her, and it fit perfectly her image of a woman leader. I will never forget that image.

Then, I met her in a more private setting, and this time, she seemed like she was of a different color, with her passion for work, her wisdom to encourage and uplift her juniors, and the joy she felt when she found a twenty dollar blouse at a department store sale. Sometimes, she seemed like the color sky-blue like cloudless autumn sky, and other times, she seemed red like the morning sun rising from the ocean. Then, there were times when she seemed green like the leaves of May. She navigates through life beautifully wearing these different colors, and all of us find great courage and strength in times of trouble from watching her.

President Huh has many joys in life. She loves to read, meet new people, and she loves exercising and doing aerobics. She fills her life with happiness and tries to share it with people around her. She is such an amazing role model, and I'm blessed to have her.

Lee Young Hee

Executive Director at KT

President Huh, I remember meeting you for the first time over ten years ago. Not only were you so talented and beautiful, you had such confidence and consideration for the underdogs. All these years, you've been a role model for all of your female juniors. I hope that you continue to shine in the future and guide us with your advice. I love you!

Park Nam Hee

Executive Director at MS

I got to know President Huh through Venture Business Women's Association seven years ago. She is one of five people in my life who inspires me and gives me motivation. The first incredible thing about her is that she maintains such unbelievable outward youth that you couldn't possibly guess her real age, which I suspect is due to her exercise habits. Watching her exercise makes me amazed at how flexible she is and at the same time, ashamed of myself for always blaming lack of time as an excuse for not exercising. The second incredible thing is the way our interactions feel so comfortable despite there being over fifteen years of age gap between us. I think this is because she is very accepting of everyone as they are and generally open-minded and considerate. Lastly, she is really sincere in her relationships with people. I believe I'm lucky to have met such an incredible person in my life.

Oh Sae Hyun

Executive Director at KT

I met President Huh for the first time at Wednesday Forum for assembly members to get educated about IT. After I got her book and began reading it, I started picturing in my mind President Huh overcoming all the obstacles and achieving one milestone after another.

When I first met her at Wednesday Forum, she opened my eyes to a new world. She was the kind of mentor I wanted to emulate. I still remember clearly how she led our meetings so smoothly, sifting through and organizing all the different opinions and assigning what we had to do for the next meeting. Through the forum, we had a chance to really contemplate on what we needed to do to advance Korean IT, and I'm grateful for this experience.

I also remember her working as the president at ICU, working to recruit foreign students and trying to bring together Korea's economy and technology.

Her advice has always been incredibly helpful to her junior colleagues. I hope this book inspires more young people in Korea to have bigger dreams and realize what they want to do in life.

Jang Hae Jung

Researcher at Korea Research Institute for
Vocational Education and Training

The admiration I felt for Dr. Huh the first time I saw her just keeps growing and growing. It knows no bounds.

When you meet professor Huh for the first time, you are immediately taken back by three things. First is her beauty and her superb figure resembling a model. Second is her superior elite educational background, and third is her great manners and presentation in all areas (her speech, sociability and her fluency in foreign languages). At first, such perfection makes you approach her with some caution and distance. For the past twenty years, I also hid my own fan-like admiration towards her when we interacted. But these days, I have finally come clean with my feelings as a proud member of our 'Huh She' group.

Interestingly, as I get to know professor Huh better and longer, there are three other things that never cease to amaze me and deepen my adoration. The first is the 'innocence' she possesses, which shows itself amidst her girlish sensibility. I think it's deeply admirable that she has achieved everything she has by relying only on her pure passion and talent, without succumbing to greed for wealth, power or status. The second thing is the fact that she is shockingly progressive despite her appearance, which gives off the 'rich Gangnam housewife' vibe. As news anchor Park Jong Jin commented, professor Huh has a sharp critical eye and left-leaning political proclivity, which still sometimes surprise me today. Lastly, professor Huh truly has a unique charm that seems to grow the more you get to know her. I have always admired her since the first time we met, and my admiration seems to keep growing endlessly. It knows no bounds.

Yoon Jung Won

CEO Uni Performance

My beautiful professor! With your girl-like innocent passion, you inspire us students to have dreams and look at the world with warmth.

Choi Mi Na

Professor at Cheongju University

"Who is that?"

"Oh, she's my professor!"

"Really? She's so cool. I wish I had a professor like that. I am jealous."

When I was in university, my male friends would see Professor Huh walk by and say that to me. They said they'd want to ask her on a date.

In those days, Dr. Huh was very stylish, with the sweater tucked-under-the jeans look. She was definitely a style icon and a noticeably beautiful and chic professor.

To all male students, she was a charismatic heartthrob of a teacher, and to female students, she was an inspiring role model who gave them dreams to look up to.

But, I believe her true charm belongs elsewhere. I think Dr. Huh's real charm is her way of thinking and working. She was a rare professor in Korean society who was always fair, reasonable, and objective and she always worked flawlessly and diligently. Dr. Huh didn't have favorites nor did she treat anyone differently for any reason. Her standards were always logical, and her evaluations were fair. With Dr. Huh, everyone had an equal opportunity to grow and learn. She created a culture of objectivity in our department and because of this, her students were able to discover their true potential and develop it.

Professor Huh is extremely talented and has many talents. The ideas she has and the results she produces are always creative, and because of this, people are usually satisfied even by her initial proposal. Despite that, she would always fix, edit, improve and upgrade everything until she was satisfied with what she had.

The first time she had interpellation session as an assembly member, she went through multiple drafts of questions to the government before she was finally satisfied the day before the session. However, that evening, she again decided to practice the speech in front of her assistant and ended up staying until very late at night changing parts that were unclear or didn't sound correct. The next morning when she came to work, her eyes were bloodshot. She'd stayed up all night practicing the speech in front of the mirror.

Even though she's in her sixties, she still maintains a girlish figure. Wherever she goes, she gains followers and admirers. Whatever job is assigned, she completes it to perfection. But I know the real secret to her brilliant and flawless self is the dedication and hard work that equal her brilliance.

In my attempt to be like her, I always ask myself, "What would Professor Huh do in this situation?" Even today.

Jung Young Ran
Professor at Seoul Digital University

As her students, we have been watching Professor Huh's life play for a long time, sometimes as actors on the stage and at other times as the audience. Each time a new act began, we were pulled in by its unpredictable storyline. The grand scale of her stories, which were often so ahead of our time, always amazed us. We were always eager to send a fervent applause when she faced tough challenges and came on top to achieve everything she wanted. Even more admirable was how humbly she laid down all of her glorious accomplishments with an innocent smile and a sense of ease instead of holding on tightly.

I would guess that in the life plays of her students, she had been the most influential actor. Had I not met her at the age of twenty-three, how different would my life have been? From whom would I have received the strength to endure all the obstacles in life? Where would I have gotten all the precious things that I now have in my life?

Through watching her life play, I can feel her spirit, her heart and her values. I can feel how deeply she loves her fellow human beings from the bottom of her heart. This book will always remain the most compelling and touching masterpiece in my life. The most amazing thing is that this work of art will not end with this book because she will go on to make further impact on her students' lives. This is the true meaning of a masterpiece.

Jung Bong Young

Dean of Global Cyber University

She's always been a role model for her students.

"I want to be a competent and confident specialist like you"

Exactly a year ago last March, my oldest daughter asked me, "Dad, what should I become when I grow up?" She was serious. To get into a prestigious top university in Korea means you need to find out your desired major early on so you can begin volunteering and building your college application portfolio from the day you enter high school. My daughter was very anxious since she hadn't discovered what she wanted to do yet. As I was thinking about how great it would be to give her a role model who could help her find her future path. The first person I thought of was Professor Huh, the best teacher I've ever had.

When I was in school, she was everyone's role model and a powerful motivator. Everyone was mesmerized by her ability, passion and beauty, and our research center always had students who came in saying, "We want to become a specialist like Dr. Huh. Please be my mentor" and who wanted her advice and letters of recommendation. Perhaps this is why students who graduated from our program while Dr. Huh was teaching became such successful professors and specialists.

This book is a quiet yet glamorous record of Professor Huh's life. But apart from telling the story of her life, it also chronicles the birth of Educational Technology as a field, development of Korea's IT industry and turmoils of Korean politics. This book shows how female leadership can change a society. Indeed, it is a book of great scale. I have been a witness to over half of the things that are described here, and I hope the younger generation today will also get a chance to read it. I hope our younger generation will learn from her passion and love of challenge. And lastly, I hope my daughter will also get to 'fly high in the sky like the clouds' and discover and go after her own dreams.

Uhm Woo Young

Professor at Keimyung University

She speaks directly and possesses charisma. She introduced Educational Technology to Korea with great foresight. She also has a sensitive and considerate side which touches people's hearts. She demonstrated great love towards her students time and again which was truly moving.

When I went to speak to her about studying abroad in the U.S., she wrote a handwritten letter for me to give to my advisor, and when she came to see me during my studies, she saw how I was struggling to raise a family and focus on my school work, and put allowance money in my palm before leaving. Later, when I went to see her with my family in Chicago during her sabbatical, she personally wrote a fun itinerary for my family so we could enjoy our trip to the fullest. All these things she did for us were deeply touching.

This is not a book that just talks about what happened in her life. It's a book that can encourage our youths to discover their own sense of adventure and passion and show why it's important to live our lives with empathy and consideration for others.

Gang Chang Gyu

CEO of Brain ID Group and Alumni President of
Educational Technology Department

This book really shows how far talent and passion can take you in life and how influential you can be in this world. Not only did Professor Huh relay knowledge to her students through the projects she worked on, she taught them to become wise and motivated them to face new challenges. She was always supportive of her students and was their cheerleader in whatever they did. Nowadays, there is less of this kind of close personal bond between professors and their students, which makes us appreciate our relationship with Professor Huh even more. Whenever our department alumni get together, we always sing the song *Pioneer*. Professor Huh always chose to walk the unfamiliar path rather than the familiar one. We, the students, have learned from this and are now living with similar passion as leaders in our own fields.

Go Dae Won · Lee Gun Gook · Noh Hyung Chul · Kim Sung Han · Kim Young Ho
Former students at ICU

President Huh has passionately devoted herself to advancing and globalizing Korea's IT industry. She is a pioneer who's always full of energy, and she's reformed and shaken up the Korean society and its educational system. The many 'firsts' she's achieved include, establishing the Educational Technology department in Korea, creating personal websites for assembly members, introducing the internet voting system and launching the International University President Forum. As entrepreneurs and scholars, we are inspired by her passion and we want to follow in her footstep and make our own contribution to our society's progress. Thank you for being the compass in the lives of your students.

Lee Hee Jung
CEO of Elics

To me, Dr. Huh represents 'motivation.' Being her student helped me gain professional credibility. Always confident, loving and proud of her students, Dr. Huh continuously motivates me to live my life the way she lives hers. I am forever thankful and proud to be her student.

Song Jung Hee
President at Korean Women in Science and Engineering

In today's fast changing world, Dr. Huh has successfully laid the foundation for Korea's information economy and helped advance its IT industry through the various roles she took, aided by her immaculate insight and superior intelligence.

In particular, the policy work she did and international diplomacy she conducted really raised Korea's prestige internationally.

Most importantly, Dr. Huh has remained an educator throughout her lifetime. She likes to share all of her knowledge with others and at times has been a moral teacher to those who act with ulterior motives and a narrow mindset.

She's always been fair to all and generous even to those who harbored ulterior agenda. She exemplifies a true leader who is both smart yet soft. I will always treasure and cherish the lessons of this book.

Lee Jung

President of Hyundai Dream Tour

My Professor Who Came to Us from the Future Through a Time Machine!

Professor Huh is my teacher, a mother to me and my wife, and a fantastic grandmother to my child.

Once when I was a senior in university, Professor Huh called me and my (now) wife to her office. When we went in, she told us, "You two should get married. I guarantee your happiness. Jung is going to do great things with his life. He's going to be big, I promise. Just get married." We were flabbergasted and amused at the moment, but some years later, we did get married. Now, I am the parent of a college student who is, majoring in IT, and who considers Dr. Huh a great mentor and a great grandma.

Dr. Huh used to make us take art as a required course. We didn't really understand the connection between Educational Technology and Art back then, but now I see how it helped me to develop a softer, warmer and artistic sensibility. Dr. Huh was a special professor who encouraged us to nurture our artistic and philosophical sides and didn't only focus on our major. One of my alumni friends even went to study more art in Japan and is now a professor in Broadcasting and Entertainment.

Educational Technology she taught was kind of a secret key into the future that she had envisioned. Listening to her lectures made us feel like we were already in a future school or corporate training. Listening to her talk was like watching a science fiction film. Hanyang graduates who are influential today owe their success to Dr. Huh and her ability to imagine the future. She is the Korean version of Alvin Toffler or Peter Druker. Actually, she is simply Huh Unna with the ability to foresee Korea's future.

Epilogue

There are times in life when other people tell my life stories. I was shocked when I read an autobiographical novel by Anita Moorjani about one woman's experience with cancer and a complete recovery called *Dying to be Me*. There was a part in the book that said, "Look at the life you lived. Why have I been so harsh on myself? Why did I always punish myself? Why didn't I realize I didn't need to be so harsh?"

When I look back at my life carefully, I have no regrets. But it's hard not to think it's true that I'd always set a certain standard for myself and lived relentlessly to live up to it. It feels like I too had been 'too harsh' with myself. I spent my youth as a 'careful and studious' child under an extremely strict grandmother, and during university years, I was determined to acquire all of the world's knowledge and refinement, which drove me to work and live tirelessly. After I moved to the States, I desperately held on to my studies as I worked with scholars from all over the world who reminded me of where I came from. After becoming a professor at FSU, I tried to execute all my projects perfectly and poured all my energy into developing research methodology. In Washington D.C.'s cutthroat world of consulting, I fought like a lonesome warrior to gain work experience and win approval. I wanted to make people see that I was 'superior to the white employees.'

After returning to Korea, my life stayed busy as I tried to help the Educational Technology field take root in Korea and help my students gain employment. And from my desire to make some kind of contribution to my country, I took on various roles as a consultant and offered my expertise whenever it was needed, and in the process, it led me to politics. During my days as a politician, I tried my best to bring some freshness to Korean politics. I gave my all to bring 'Silly Roh Mu Hyun' to presidency, and after leaving politics, I was again flying east and west to produce young IT talents who will lead Korea and raise its status in the world. After turning sixty, I lowered my sails in Songdo and dedicated myself to educating young leaders, imagining a better future for Korea's education and living a life of service as an educator.

Once when I was in school in the States, I took a class on the theory of societal change. From that class, the concept of 'change agent' remained in my memory forever. And looking back, I think I really embraced that role throughout my life.

Living with others, you sometimes hear bad gossip and there are inevitable misunderstandings. Conflicts happen. When I was young, there were incidents where someone would come up to me and tell me, "So and so is talking badly about you." Whenever this happened, I would tell them, "Please don't ever share these things with me." When you hear negative rumors, you feel bad, and eventually you will try to meet with that person to sort the misunderstanding. I felt like this was a lot of wasted time and a distraction from my work that I needed to do. So, I decided early on that I wouldn't explain myself to those who didn't understand me. Instead, I'd spend that time focusing on things that really mattered to me and things that were right, and hoped people would know my truth over time. I realized that to have the love and recognition of everyone is impossible and decided not to answer back to any rumors to justify myself.

Perhaps this fanned the flames to a lot of the jealousy, envy and misunderstandings that surrounded me when I was younger. For a while, my nickname was 'Leave it alone' because whenever a professor would come to me and say, "This person did this wrong" or "This person's problem is this," I would tell them to "leave it alone." I don't really like to pick apart people's small flaws or mistakes. For the most part, I prefer to overlook them. My 'apathetic' or 'stand-offish' attitude created a lot of misperceptions about me, but there were also advantages. I managed to bypass a lot of relationship problems with people, and I think this was fortunate.

In a way, I am really enjoying my age now because I can put everything down and be freer. Yes, sometimes, this approach forces me to live a more lonely life, but perhaps, that is the life given to a shaker, mover, and a pioneer. Most people live their lives hanging in groups, but I went through each stage of my life driven by a sense of duty, which propelled me to move forward, and I often took a path that others couldn't well understand. People always saw me leading and initiating projects and events. This image may have seemed glamorous, but in reality, I usually felt lonely because I was always the only person who was responsible for producing the results and executing all the plans.

Once, I wanted to understand my loneliness more deeply and came across this wise excerpt from the Chinese novel, *The Art of War* (孫子兵法) in chapter 6, 虛實 (voidness vs. fullness).

> Sun Tzu (孫子) once said that one should work like the river. The water flows from higher altitude to low, lowering itself to pass the opponent's solidity and discern their weaknesses. One should be adaptable to different situations, water changes its flows depending on geography and doesn't insist on a particular shape. One should be able to change one's strategies to lead oneself to victory. This is the truly ghostly level of victory.

This excerpt really outlined how important it is for a leader to be flexible and humble when facing grave matters. It also stresses that a single victory doesn't guarantee future victories, so a leader should be ready to change their ways endlessly depending on each situation.

The excerpt is about the importance of creativity, but it also implies the loneliness a leader must accept and endure since they should always be ready to forge new a path. Comparing this to my life, I don't think I've ever had a victory that was truly 'ghostly.' However, I did always reach for new ways and in going through with them, I always tried to keep an open and flexible mind and keep my eyes and ears wide open. I also pride myself in knowing that through it all, I always stayed humble towards learning new things from any situation.

Throughout my life, I've had to embrace my loneliness as life's companion as my life was always filled with new challenges. I think I figured out early on that life itself is loneliness.

Even though I think to myself, "I've done enough. I've made my contribution to society and brought some needed changes and reforms," sometimes, that others don't recognize this makes me feel ashamed. The excerpt from the novel gave me comfort because it showed most people don't ever see how victories and great accomplishments came to be.

People usually understand how their leaders accomplished a great feat only after a long time has passed. This has always been true. 2500 years ago, Sun Tsu understood this loneliness that leaders have to bear. I try to comfort myself by telling myself I am feeling the same feelings he felt. Maybe this is the reason why so many people study the classics.

Over the years, I have received so much love and help from many people. But I never had the chance to give back to them. And I'm afraid that I may never have the chance to. My biggest weakness is my inability to remember people's faces and names. There have been more than a few occasions where I disappointed my supporters by not recognizing them when I met them in person. I would like to take this opportunity to bow my head low and thank all my students from Hanyang and ICU, my supporters from Bundang and many businessmen and women working in IT, politics, academia and industries who have helped and loved me. I feel I owe each one of them huge debt and hope to repay their kindness by continuing to love and support my juniors. It's comforting to know that I can still do that.

The famous expression in show business is, "The show must go on."

It means that no matter what happens, the show must be performed for the sake of its audience. A show or a play is only meaningful when it is performed. My life's 8 acts and 23 scenes don't end here. The stories that will come after this play will be drastically different, and I'll be different from my present self, but the play is still in progress even in this very moment. I am curious to see where it will lead and believe there are still 'roads less traveled' waiting for me to choose them. A new path of service, a road full of unexpected adventure, and now with age, a more relaxed and less lonely road, I am still looking forward to my new undefined road with a fluttering heart.